DIALOGUE

DIALOGUE

The State of the Church Today

ROSEMARY HAUGHTON

and

CARDINAL HEENAN

SHEED AND WARD : NEW YORK

First published 1967
© 1967 Geoffrey Chapman Ltd

This book is set in 11 pt on 13 pt Intertype Plantin
Made and printed in Great Britain

Contents

Preface

We did not meet until February 1967. We were drawn together by a common love for the Church of God and a common anxiety about the future of the Church in England, in particular about the lack of understanding between members of the laity and the hierarchy. It was while we were wondering what could be done to bring about a better relationship, so that the Church might, as a whole, follow God's call with single-minded confidence, that we had the idea of collaborating. We may achieve nothing but we think the attempt worth making.

Prefaces are usually almost an afterthought of the author when a book has been completed. This preface was composed before either of us had decided exactly what to write. Perhaps we ought first to apologise for the title we have chosen. If any word is worked to death it is 'dialogue'. Yet we chose this title quite deliberately because it seemed the clearest statement of intention. That is why we feel we ought to offer the reader some explanation.

Running second to 'dialogue' as an all-purpose word in the current jargon is 'communication'. Disputes between members of the Church are often attributed to lack of communication. More communication can, of course, make people like each other even less, but lack of communication fosters misunderstanding, and misunderstanding is the most

common cause of disagreements. The removal of misunderstanding cannot alone produce brotherly love, but it can
make understanding possible, so that love has a chance to
grow.

Our plan is to divide the book into four sections. The first
will give a layman's view of the present situation in the
Church and both fears and hopes for the future. The second
will be a bishop's reflection on the post-conciliar scene.
(Neither will be a statement of policy. The second section
will not purport to represent the views of the hierarchy any
more than the first will claim to be the official voice of the
laity.) The third and fourth sections will be our commentaries on each other's views. These will not be polemical.
They will be dialectic without setting out to prove each other
wrong. That would be a denial of dialogue.

The object of our discussion is to bring out into the open
the anxieties and hopes felt by the people of God in all walks
of life. Differences in religious outlook are widened and
hardened by failure to study another point of view. The same
is true of political differences. The man who reads only that
literature which gives the views of his own party will never
learn anything good about his opponents. Nothing can more
effectively block the work of the Spirit in the Church than
the banding together of one group against another. On the
other hand, open and generous disagreement and discussion
can and does lead to greater knowledge and love, to the development of fruitful ideas and to the true unity of God's
people.

We set out on our dialogue without conscious prejudice. It
is not our intention to put each other right. Each of us is in
close touch with Catholics whose attitudes have grown
mutually more estranged with every passing crisis, but we
know that disharmony within the Church in England is not

a battle between priests and laymen. There is no lack of anti-clerical clergy, while a considerable number of laity grieve at the criticism of ecclesiastical authority. Nor do we think that there is any clear difference between the well educated and the poorly educated. The ill-educated are largely unaware of the nature of the disputes in progress within the Church, but are made uneasy by an atmosphere of uncertainty.

We hope to examine together certain questions of some urgency. Why do some 'intellectuals' attack the Holy See and the hierarchy? Are the bishops too rigid in their attitudes? Are they blocking the road to freedom and reform? Is their prudence really a mask for fear? Is there any danger of anarchy in the Church? Has obedience ceased to be a virtue? And, beyond all these questions, what is the will of God for the Church? Which way is the Holy Spirit pushing the people of God in this century?

These questions cannot be finally answered but our hope is to encourage all God's people to come together for discussion. It is time for warm-hearted dialogue, undertaken in the confidence that when we call on God to send his Holy Spirit, so that in us he may renew the face of the earth, we are not reciting an empty formula. Out of doubt and suspicion and fear a new birth can come, if we are prepared to listen to the Spirit, and in our turn to speak the word of God that is in us.

Rosemary Haughton
John Cardinal Heenan

One

Rosemary Haughton

An unchanging Church?

The Catholic Church is troubled, and the trouble began with
the Council. All the questions that plague Catholics now are
being aired because the Council made it possible to ask such
questions, and not in a whisper. All the doubts, as well as
the hopes, start there, all the unrest, and the disagreements,
as well as the reforms, grow from that huge gathering of the
world's Catholic bishops. None of the things these bishops
discussed were unheard of before, some were familiar to the
point of boredom, but the Council gathered up and gave a
voice to all the ideas and ideals that had been stirring in the
Church for decades. At last it seemed possible that something could be done. The giant did not merely stir in his
sleep as he dreamed. He sat up and blinked and looked
around. And the world at large, long accustomed to the giant
who slept with such definity and such confidence of never
being disturbed, saw this awakening. It was almost as surprised as the giant himself. But there were shocks in store
for both, and not all of them were pleasant ones.

There were many who doubted the wisdom of awakening
the giant. But awake he did.

When the Council began there were some people who felt it was unnecessary, or even a great mistake. But most Catholics who thought about it at all were glad, even excited. And to some it was a huge relief because of the pressure of new ideas that had not been able to find an outlet. But whatever the variations of enthusiasm and the reasons for it, there was the feeling that, suddenly, the Church was at the beginning of a new era and anything might happen.

Even so, what has in fact happened has taken most of us by surprise. It is as if one began to tidy a workshop, to make room for new and more efficient tools, and the effort to make room for them revealed not only that the tidying would have to be absolutely radical but even that perhaps the workshop itself needed redesigning if it was to be useful for the new work.

The opinions that came to the surface at the Council were not all new, they had already been developing for some time —in some cases for several decades—but many of the ideas had until then been tentative and unformulated. They were there, however, and very strong. It was urgently necessary that they should be allowed expression if they were not to blow the Church to bits. But very few people realized what would happen once the reorganizing got going. The Church had been apparently unchanging for so long that most people took it for granted that to be unchanging was an essential mark of the Church. At most, an energetic tidying up could be necessary. All kinds of people responded happily to the idea of renewing the life of the Church because it simply didn't seem possible that anything so massively continuous as the Catholic Church could be shaken. It would be a matter of tidying up, clearing, rearranging, so that everything would be clear and easily available. Then life would go on as before, only better.

It is true that there were many—especially the younger

theologians—who saw more clearly what might be involved, but even for them the past had a soothing and comforting effect. And to the vast majority any disturbing upheaval was quite unimaginable when the Council began. Looking back, now, we can see how feeble our sense of history must have been. The unchangingness of the Church is a fairly recent thing, a matter of a few hundred years. Taking a longer view it is clear that the Church has suffered cataclysmic changes in its history, and that our cosy nineteenth century confidence is very local indeed.

If one reads St Augustine, for instance, his writing reflects a Church torn by fierce and powerful heresies, in a society still largely pagan, in which Christians were not remarkable for sobriety. Dioceses were scarcely larger than modern parishes, bishops could be chosen by public acclaim, the emperor—though Christian—was still semi-divine in influence if not in theory, and was also often a heretic, as were many of the bishops.

In the 'dark ages' it was the monasteries that preserved the faith and preached it, converting and civilizing the barbarous northern nations. European Christianity was kept in being by the network of monasteries, great and small. The bishops' role was comparatively uninfluential, though essential. The king was the spiritual head of his people, symbol of the whole nation: in a sense he *was* the people, and the conversion of a king meant the conversion of a people.

In the middle ages the picture was different again. Emperors were now comparatively powerless, and were less powerful than the pope, whose rule was supreme. Heresy was widespread and fervent, but persecuted: the hierarchy of the Church was immensely powerful; nation states were beginning to emerge, and were often governed, in practice, by clerics.

Changes of this order alter the picture so much that it

might be hard to realize that there was any real continuity
at all. The continuity lies in the mission and purpose of the
Church, struggling to express itself in vastly different circumstances. It is the mission that does not change; but also,
because of that mission, a certain kind of arrangement of
people as a community comes about, in order that the mission can be understood by succeeding generations, and faith-
fully handed on. This is the natural human pattern of
authority, such as always occurs when a group of people are
trying *both* to be a community, in the present, *and* to make
it possible for the community to continue having the same
essential 'personality' and purpose in the future.

All this we can see now, but it was not so easy to see it in
the early days of the Council. The almost euphoric confidence
that many people felt in the work of the Council was only
partly due to a proper Christian trust in the power of the
Spirit to guide the Church. It was at least partly the result
of this lack of historical sense, so that it never occurred to us
that the changes might be as totally revolutionary as Pentecost itself. We listened happily when Pope John described
the Council as the occasion of a 'new Pentecost', but few
stopped to realize that the first Pentecost was an event that
turned all previous religion inside out, superseded the law,
and laid mankind wide open to the Spirit. And the Spirit of
God is not a domestic central-heating system, but a blazing
fire.

Is spring-cleaning enough?
So what happened was that in the course of the Council it
became clear to everyone who paid attention that if the clearing out and cleaning and renewing were undertaken with real
energy there was no very clear limit to the changes that
might be effected. To some this was a liberating and inspir-
ing idea, to others it was a threat.

To Catholics who followed the progress of the Council debates, as they were 'leaked' to the press in increasing volume and with increasing confidence, what was happening seemed scarcely believable. If the French revolution had seemed so great a liberation that people really felt 'Bliss was it in that dawn to be alive, But to be young was very heaven', then the unbloody revolution being hatched in St Peter's certainly could make people feel that heaven was possible. But, bloody or not, it was a revolution that was beginning, though its planners scarcely realized it. And some people were not happy about it. In fact, some were horrified. They genuinely felt that the Church was in danger of capitulating to the secular world in a misguided attempt to move with the times. To these people Pope John was a simple-minded idealist who, in his ignorance, was opening the gates to the forces of materialism and atheism. Their idea of the Church's nature and mission was one that had been formed by the centuries following the Reformation, when Catholicism was on the defensive, and striving to preserve its integrity and sense of purpose by a fierce emphasis on unity, obedience and an unchanging traditional structure. To question any of these seemed to be to question the very existence of Catholicism.

Of course these people were right. Once you start asking questions it is not easy to stop. Fresh answers to one set of questions provoke new and more radical questions about the same things, and other things (just as the clearing of one shelf reveals the need for more and more back-breaking work, and threatens to disrupt the whole routine of the household for an indefinite period). The people who dreaded the effects of the Council were more far-seeing than most because they realized, for example, that to ask questions about the language of the liturgy would lead in the end to asking questions about the whole liturgical idea, and even about the Eucharist itself. They knew that to lower the denominational barriers an inch would mean, in the long run, a reappraisal of the theological issues that divide Christians in order to see if they really *do* divide or are only made to do so because we *want* our divisions. They saw that if the Church really opened its heart to the non-Christian world, to the scientists and atheists and communists, then sooner or later Catholics would begin to take seriously not only the souls of non-Christians but their ideas also, because you can't separate people from their thinking. All this could only lead people to wonder, at last, why the Church existed at all, and whether it was simply an historical phenomenon that had given good service but must now disappear.

All these fears have been justified, and those who entertained them have been proved much wiser than those of us who were certain that reform could proceed without risk of revolution. A translated and simpler liturgy, a theology presented in present-day language, removal of petty and out-of-date restrictions, close ties with other denominations, a sane and charitable appreciation of those ideas from non-Christian sources that are of value to the modern Church— these things are what most of us hoped for, during and just after the Council. We believed that if all this came about the new spirit of Pope John would begin to work in the Church.

The 'layers' of Catholic response to the Council

This was not, in fact, what happened. A process once started must go on. Or at least there is a possibility of its going on, and there is no clearly marked point at which it seems possible to stop. By the end of the Council then, and for a little while afterwards, the situation of Catholic thinking (in the European tradition, that is) was divided up somewhat like this:

There were the dug-in traditionalists, of varying degrees of intelligence and piety, who agreed, at all levels, in regretting the Council, condemning change and fearing for the future of Christianity.

There were the moderate Council enthusiasts who felt that the door was open, that much could be accomplished in time, that reform would indeed revive failing popular interest, make possible Christian reunion sometime (not very soon) and strengthen the Church's mission to the world.

There were the whole-hearted Council enthusiasts to whom Vatican II was like a vision of heaven opened. They saw a Church purified, free of fear and of the burden of material cares, open to all men and to truth wherever it occurred. It was an eschatological vision, God's kingdom on earth. How it could possibly happen wasn't an important question. It was a call from God, he would see to the rest.

There were a few who thought that in fact reform was self-doomed, because if it was pushed far enough it could only reveal the basic inadequacy of the inherited Catholic set-up to the tasks of the century—liturgically, theologically and structurally. Reform, in fact, could only be a futile prelude to revolution, if the Church was to face up to the modern world, philosophically, politically and spiritually.

There was also, besides all these, the vast majority who scarcely realized that the Council was going on. They continued much as before and learned to answer at Mass, first in Latin and then in English, with the same docility with which they had previously recited the rosary before Benediction. Rome was a long way off, geographically and spiritually. What mattered, in making religion important or not, was the quality of the priests who served them and of the other Christians they knew.

None of these groups could easily be characterized according to class or profession or level of education, nor did the clerical-lay division act as a simple test, though naturally the clergy were more likely to realize that *something* was going on, because they had to explain it to others. (Even so, there were some who stuck to the bare announcement of changes, not always from disapproval but sometimes from sheer inability to make sense of it all.) It was natural to think that the less educated would be less interested, and largely this was true. The older people tended to be less enthusiastic, too. But there were many fierce conservatives among the teenagers and the intellectuals. There were revolutionaries among the elderly, and there was an uneducated old woman of over eighty (surely not unique) who wrote that now she understood what the Council was doing she thanked God for allowing her to live long enough to see it happen.

A changed situation

That was not so very long ago. In many ways the situation is still the same, these broad divisions still apply; but there has been a change of atmosphere. An enormous amount is being done, there have been achievements that would have seemed incredible a few years ago; yet in spite of this there is a very rapid deterioration in some respects, a restlessness and a sense of disillusion. The change has been epitomized as a 'crisis of authority' and this description may be either true and revealing, or distorted and narrow, according to the way in which authority is understood: according to the way in which one understands the idea of authority, one interprets the present situation as hopeful or disastrous.

What is this situation? What has changed? What are the signs that something is wrong? And are the signs really signs of something *wrong*?

One thing has not changed. The attitude of the ultra-conservatives is unaltered, unless it has hardened. They have no reason to change. They *know* what the Church is, and all their fears for it have proved to be well grounded.

Another group has not so much changed as developed and

grown stronger and more convinced. These are the people who realize that a new Pentecost means a revolution, not a tidying up. They welcome the questioning of everything, because it is only by questioning ruthlessly that what is truly essential can be revealed, perhaps in so strange a form that at first it is unrecognizable. Some of those who pursue the kind of study that this involves find that it has to be done in such a specialized way, because of the newness of the ideas and language, as to remain a theoretical and separated pursuit. Not all agree with them, and in any case this is becoming less true: the growing influence of the way of thinking typified by the *Slant* group is not only due to accidental publicity or the alleged 'noisiness' of its members. It is not mere cussedness that makes people seize on Marxist language to re-express Christian ideas. This approach can easily become a gimmick but it is, basically and in spite of mistakes and lack of balance, part of something so deeply and importantly Christian as to be hard to recognize or accept just because it is so fundamental. I shall return to this later, but at this point it is useful to notice that people who think like this are not all 'intellectuals', meaning highly educated people who are able, by training, to analyse and express accurately the feelings and ideas that other people work out rather in action and scarcely articulate living. The interesting thing is to notice how people with no philosophical language very often express in their own terms the same 'feel' for the quality of modern life that the 'intellectuals' write about. And when the two meet, they get on well.

They don't get on well with the moderate Council enthusiasts, who are among those who have suffered greatly from the development of the present crisis. It is clear that things are not working out as they had hoped, and there is a general atmosphere of disillusion. People don't go to Benediction as much as they used to, but they don't exactly flock to Mass,

even in the evenings. After the novelty of English in the
liturgy has worn off the general set-up seems much the same.
Inter-church relations are cordial, but there is a growing
sense of anti-climax. The question in the ecumenical field is
beginning to be, 'What is a united Church *for*?' The nuns
who modernized their habits and their rules are beginning to
wonder whether under the new habit and rule there is a real
life, or whether religious life itself is as dated as the old dress.
Not all allow such questions to rise to the surface and be
asked, but nearly all feel the uneasiness, the doubt, the lessening of confidence. The same malaise is eroding the enthusiasm
of many Catholic organizations, and their membership either
falls or grows older and older. The ones that survive best are
those concerned with direct practical action, whose useful-
ness is clear by any standards. Their members tend to be
largely unaware of the doubts and tensions undermining
Catholic life. Yet, all the same, they are affected by them.
They may not know what is wrong, but they do know that
something is, and their anxious questions betray bewilderment that other Catholics seem to be so odd and difficult to
talk to. For one effect of the lack of confidence among the
moderates is to make people draw away from each other.

The birth control question

Among the factors which have most deeply undermined the
hope and confidence of the moderate Catholics the birth
control issue has probably been the most important. For the
very conservative the question is a closed one, for the ultra-
progressive it has been solved. And the huge mass of uneducated Catholics agonize and compromise and struggle heroically and accept defeat philosophically, and get what help they
can from the clergy, much as they have always done. (The
difference for them arises from the differences in clerical attitudes to the subject.) But the many middle class Catholics

who welcomed the Council and settled down happily to try to co-operate in making it effective have been badly hit. It is true that the miseries of Catholic married couples over the ban on contraception certainly did not begin with the Council. But when there seemed to be no possible question about the Church's teaching the matter was at least clear-cut. Either you obeyed and stayed in, at least until illness and mental breakdown made religion irrelevant anyway, or else you couldn't face it and got out—quietly and miserably or defiantly and noisily. What has now made the situation almost unbearable is the sense of hope deferred. The apparently closed question was reopened. Whatever anybody said about it, that was what happened as far as ordinary people were concerned. Books, articles, letters in the newspapers, all discussed the question, and it was clear that nearly all those who wrote about it were convinced that the traditional teaching on contraception was not unalterable, and that it would be altered. Advice given in the confessional varied from a total and absolute ban, with refusal of absolution as sanction, to assurances that no ban existed. People exchanged experiences, and afterwards changed confessors. But still nothing definite happened, there was no clear statement of freedom to decide. Some struggled with 'rhythm' for years, sometimes successfully, and looked back wearily, wondering whether all the heartache and bitterness had been really necessary. The less fortunate suddenly concluded that estrangement and ill-health had been imposed on them in the name of God's law, and reacted by violent repudiation of what had come to seem a callous system. Many couples used contraceptives and either did, or didn't, go to the sacraments, but kept quiet about it. In any case, and in all the variations of practice or non-practice, defiance or compliance, the overall atmosphere created by this situation was one of rapidly lessening respect for the teaching authority of Church, conceived as a repository of once-for-all clear-cut directives. It was hard to feel any great enthusiasm for the renewal of the Church when an acute personal problem overshadowed everything. Besides, the Church that one was told one had to renew seemed to be in a state of complete dither about that problem. Its authorities could only utter soothing noises interspersed with pronouncements that were meant to sound authoritative but were in fact carefully worded so as to say nothing. There have been other reasons for the increasing lack of conviction among ordinary Catholics of goodwill, but this one has almost certainly been the most important. It has been the most important because nothing else seemed more important. And this is a measure of the ineffectiveness of renewal as it presented itself to many people. When people are deeply absorbed in some worthwhile undertaking their sexual life, though important, takes second place. But if there is nothing of overriding importance then sex matters much more, because sex is real and warm, it is about love, about people. It is a real sharing, a making of the community of marriage. Most people can easily and happily do without sex for a good reason—for instance if their husband or wife is ill. But Catholics felt they were being asked to give up one really good and human thing for *no* reason that anyone could explain convincingly. And to call the alternative 'obedience', whether to God or the Church, did *not* provide a reason, but merely brought into question the meaning of God and the Church.

The result of all this is not only a constant trickle of people leaving the Church. It is also a pervasive depression, a sense of futility which is to be met with in many different kinds of gatherings. It is not by any means confined to the birth control question alone, but this factor is often the underlying one. When lay people of like background get together, after a parent-teacher session, for instance, or at a parish jumble sale, or after a Newman lecture, the atmosphere of cynicism or of genial hopelessness is very marked. It is true that 'things' are happening, much is being achieved, but in spite of this the general feeling is 'it won't happen', and 'it' is some hope, scarcely formulated perhaps, that was encouraged by the Council but is gradually dying. And the reason why 'it won't happen' is always the same: 'they won't allow it'. 'They' are the bishops, and sometimes the Vatican. (It is interesting that very few people blame the Pope, personally.) A cynicism that grows out of continued bewilderment and lack of a sense of direction is one of the most marked symptoms. It affects particularly some of the clergy, who joke about the subjects on which they feel most uneasy, in order to hide their basic spiritual disintegration. The old certainties have gone, and among all the arguments and directives nothing clearly shows the way ahead. And this is true even of people who have worked hard and successfully to 'put the Council into practice' in whatever ways were possible in their immediate surroundings.

All these people are the moderate 'progressives' (if one must use these dreadful words). They are a very great number of lay people and clergy, of all levels of means and education, who do not expect to achieve anything spectacular but who keep the Church going. Their loyalty and willingness, or lack of them, determine the quality of the Church as a cultural entity, crossing and uniting the cultural layers of the wider national society. If their morale is bad then the Church's health is threatened, and at the moment they are certainly not in a robust condition.

Those who saw a vision
Emerging from this group, and not clearly marked off from it in any way, are those Catholics who are definitely and

whole-heartedly enthusiastic about the task the Council proposed to the Church. These people are committed, to use another overworked word. They are not necessarily better educated, but as far as the affairs of the Church are concerned they are better informed because they are more deeply interested. To them the Council offered a vision of the Church that transformed their Christian lives. Fired by a new hope they studied and worked, seizing every opportunity that occurred, and expected that these opportunities would rapidly increase. These people are politically of many shades of opinion and they do not necessarily agree about either the methods or the speed of renewal, but they are united in more than ordinary love for the Church and mankind. They include a very large number of clergy and religious, and the laymen are often either professional people or people active in trade unions or voluntary organizations. They are the people, in fact, who must take the lead in the renewal of Christian life throughout the Church.

These are the people who have been hardest hit by disillusion. Because they care more and hope more they find disappointment harder to bear. The breadth of vision opened by the Council made it possible for them to realize ways in which the life of the Church could rediscover itself and be effective in the world in a manner scarcely imaginable ten years ago. They longed for a new people, drawing its life from a fully intelligible and fully shared liturgy; a community involved in all the sufferings and hopes of the world, and prepared to put aside all restrictions that prevented this involvement. They saw all around them problems and miseries, national and world-wide, that Catholics *could* help to relieve, and above all could *share*, thereby bringing the light of Christ into the dark places that needed it most.

In many cases this terrific surge of hope was unrealistic. It did not take into account the amount of work involved in making changes affecting millions. It did not allow for the inbred cautiousness of administration, or the difficulty of changing rooted attitudes. And often people who cared particularly about one special field of reform got the thing out of proportion. Also, the passion for freedom and progress made people (especially young ones) under-estimate the need for continuity in a community if it is to hold together. But, unrealistic or not, these desires, this impatience, were the result of a genuine Christian impulse, the driving power of the Spirit. This was mixed, naturally, with personal ambition, with dislike of sameness and drudgery, with impatience of people who seemed less enthusiastic, with arrogance and iconoclasm. But this is the normal human mixture, and the work of grace is gradually to set free the genuine impulse of the Spirit from all that might hinder it. This process is one that takes time and understanding and a great deal of love, and it is easily distorted or prevented.

These people, the natural leaders of the Church, are now suffering a great deal. Their hopes are constantly deferred, their initiatives squashed, their appeals for help refused, their ideas ignored. Those who have achieved most are often aware that their achievement is always under threat of destruction. I don't in the least want to minimize what has been achieved—the new parish councils, and even diocesan priests' councils, generally helping to 'run' the Church democratically; the experiments that have been encouraged or allowed; the new spurt of hope and of self-sacrifice. But what has been and is being done is not irreversible. And it is very 'patchy'. Too many, in spite of all this, feel an encroaching depression.

In many cases it is necessary to know such people personally in order to realize the extent of their suffering. They are slow to express grievances because they are not primarily interested in themselves but in their work. So, young priests will struggle for years to carry out the work that needs doing, and never rebel openly at restrictions and indifference and criticism from superiors, because they feel the work is worth doing as long as it can be done. The same applies to nuns and to lay people. But any prolonged discussion in a sympathetic group reveals a deep frustration leading often to a rooted bitterness and cynicism. It is true that those who are most fully Christian can and do grow spiritually through suffering like this. In the end it may well be that their pain will be fruitful for their work, and the results they are denied will be apparent later. But people who have learned to accept frustration and failure and grow by it are people who have been formed in courage and sacrifice by the love which they have found in the Church. In whatever way it was mediated to them it was the love of Christ which they recognized and to which they responded. People grow in love by being loved, and it is a commonplace of psychology that people who are unloved, untrusted and insecure are apt to be suspicious, resentful, aggressive and withdrawn. The impulse of generosity is not hard to stimulate momentarily, but if it is to become more than an added source of faintly nostalgic cynicism the impulse has to be sustained by sympathy and encouragement. And over and over again it is these that have been lacking.

If one travels about the country it is tragic to realize the sense of isolation and hopelessness that haunts some of the most enthusiastic, even though there are countless others who share their ideals and their hopes. This feeling of disillusion exists alongside, and in spite of, huge positive achievements in the work of renewal. It is a strange contradiction that so much good work is being done, and yet the sense of frustration grows. The reason for it is very largely the lack of contact between people doing pioneering work, and the lack of any feeling that what is being achieved is recognized as significant by the official leaders of the Church (with wonderful exceptions).

The effects of frustrated hope

This frustration affects people in different ways, according to temperament. Some struggle on, immersing themselves in the work and trying not to think much outside it. This is possible especially if the work is mainly practical, like work for the poor or teaching. Even here the further it develops as a Christian work the more it is bound to challenge traditional liturgical and theological formulations. When the work is directly concerned with the effort to create a real Christian community, with the study or teaching of theology and with religious formation at all levels, then it very soon begins to push against its present limits, and it becomes increasingly hard to avoid the challenge they present. Beyond a certain point the ability to work within the given framework demands either immense resources of courage and patience and hope, or else an interior abdication of responsibility, which inevitably lessens the effectiveness of what *is* done.

But in order to summon up all one's reserves of patience, take a long view, and carry on, it is necessary to be very certain that the limitations imposed are really necessary, at least temporarily. This means that at the moment it is not only the naturally impatient and fiery who begin to protest publicly as well as among friends, but also those whose devotion to the people of God will not allow them to accept limitations to work that so clearly needs doing, unless they have *proved* the necessity of such limitations. And the only way to do that is to keep on pushing at the present limitations, in spite of disapproval and discouragement, until one comes up against final opposition.

When this happens, some people leave the Church, because the reform they are working for seems more vital than the reasons given for preventing it. No one but God can weigh motives and judge consciences, but there is no doubt that many are leaving the Church as a direct result of the work of the Council. This is happening because the Council opened up new horizons and encouraged people to explore. When their explorations are checked—arbitrarily, so it seems to them, and without understanding—then they find it hard to believe that such a limiting of Christian effort (as they see it) *can* be true to the demands of the Spirit at this time. An organization that can so frustrate a genuine desire for truth and community no longer seems a credible witness to Christ. Whether they are likely to find such a witness elsewhere is another matter.

The majority do not react like this. There are many who show an enormous capacity for absorbing disappointment without becoming bitter, but who, even so, find the edge of their enthusiasm blunted in time. Bashing at a brick wall is not a good use for fine instruments. But there are also some who neither leave the Church nor accept disappointment. They fight. They demand the reforms they feel are necessary and when these are refused they publicize their grievances in Catholic periodicals and papers, and also in national ones if that seems likely to be effective. They fight at the theoretical level and also at the practical one, because they have a fierce assurance of the reality and urgency of the Church's mission, and an equally fierce indignation at anything, internal or external, that seems to be preventing it. This anger and pugnacity spring, ultimately, not from any pleasure in destruction or in conflict but from the extreme clarity of the vision of the Church which they see. (This vision was made possible by the Council, even when a number of those who see it are impatient of some of the Council documents that appear to be half-hearted compromises with the past.) But when the pursuit of their vision is blocked the energy of the pursuit turns to anger, and anger can settle down into a matter-of-fact negativeness that takes it for granted that all opposition is the result of stupidity or dishonesty or timidity, or all three. This is not an attractive or Christian state of mind, but it happens because real enthusiasm, real commitment to Christian renewal, has lacked the conditions of proper growth, which asks not necessarily unlimited freedom but reasonable freedom, combined with the confidence that comes from being trusted. Trust breeds patience, generosity and humility. Distrust breeds arrogance, shrill defensiveness, cynicism, and a recklessness that will use any method of attack to break through the opposition. Even when things haven't reached this pitch, to be constantly treated as potentially disloyal and untrustworthy provokes the reaction that is so common in adolescents—exaggeration, habitual over-statement, defiance, as a way of making oneself heard in the face of grown-up smugness. I am not suggesting that highly intelligent grown-up people should be considered as if they were adolescents, but that when people are *treated* like adolescents their emotions are similar to those of adolescents with not very perceptive parents, and are expressed in equivalent ways for equivalent reasons. It would be a great mistake, however, to assume that all violent or strongly critical statement is an exaggeration, or evidence of rashness, immaturity or lack of balance, however understandable. Some of it is the only adequate reaction to the failures of God's people to respond to God's call. Jeremiah was far more insulting than any modern critic of the Church, John the Baptist wasn't exactly conciliatory in his attitude to the official guardians of religion, and the things Dante said about the Church of his time make Herbert McCabe's comments look like flattery. In truth, there is never a time when the Church can absolve herself from the charges that such men make, and it is a sign of health if they can be uttered. If the Church is corrupt—and there never was a time when she was not—then someone has to say so, say where the corruption lies and what needs to be done about it. The attitude that is really disloyal is not that of these accusers, but that of the one who, knowing that the Church is suffering from wounds inflicted by her own sins, will pour in her wounds neither wine to cleanse, nor oil to soothe, but prefers to keep his hands clean, passing by on the other side rather than be soiled by the touch of a Body lying in the mess of mud and blood.

The 'simple faithful'

Among and behind and beyond those Catholics who understand in *some* degree what is going on in the Church, and react to it in any number of different ways, there are those enigmatic characters 'the simple faithful'. They are sometimes spoken of as if their 'simplicity' were an innate quality of mind or heart that must be accepted. Who are they, really?

They are the Catholics, of *all* levels of general education and intelligence, who are *theologically* uneducated. Their religious knowledge is inadequate to vanishing point; they have no equipment, therefore, with which to assess the nature of the changes in the Church and judge them. Therefore these changes reach them as an unintelligible but definite alteration in the religious 'climate' in which they have lived. What had seemed certain and immovable (even if sometimes only marginally relevant) is clearly not as solid as it seemed. Where before there was at least a rock, either to be supported by or to kick against, there is a shifting fog. Their 'simplicity' consists mainly in the fact that their religion has been content to express itself in certain simple and fixed formulae of belief and behaviour. These are often the expression of a very real, strong and deep faith, but the formulation cannot convey the variety or depth of their commitment. Such a 'simplicity' can be undermined by an atmosphere in which these formulae appear less certain and reliable, and it is being so undermined at present. There is an unease, a puzzled resignation or a cynical shedding of what now appears to have been a comfortable illusion—and sometimes sheer, blatant misery.

The natural reaction of the better informed to this is to want to protect people from a huge hurt against which they have no defence. This is a very right feeling, but it is unrealistic. The fact is that nobody, however simple, can be protected from the knowledge that the Church is in a state of upheaval. It is reflected in the Catholic press and in the national press, it is present in the words and even the tone of voice of well-informed people, it filters through the grille of the confessional, it resounds in the Sunday sermon. And attempts to protect by withholding information or offering cheerful explanations only make things worse, because the simple faithful are not *that* simple. They know they are being offered soft soap and they suffer even more from this lack of trust than they do from the evidences of trouble.

This is a perfectly familiar situation in a family. If there is trouble between—or for—the parents, the children know it. They may have no idea what is wrong, but they are not taken in by attempts to pretend that all is well. They suffer from being shut out, from uncertainty and fear of the unknown. The remedy is not to hide the truth but to tell it. Even quite young children respond magnificently if they are told the truth of a situation. Even if they do not fully understand, they know they are trusted. Instead of being on the outside, threatened but helpless, they *belong*, they are part of the situation and can do something to help. They may suffer—but this suffering is a challenge and an opportunity, and anyone who has seen children carrying, undismayed, the burden of an appalling family situation can only celebrate the glory of human love and heroism. If *children* can respond like this, grown-up Christians can do so even more. Provided they are trusted.

This sketch of Catholic thought and feeling at the present time is inevitably far too general and lacking in detail, but it does, I think, give a fair picture of the overall situation. If it seems sombre, this is not because nothing is being achieved. Rather the reverse—positive progress breeds hope, and hope deferred or disappointed is the real cancer of the spirit. There is one symptom that appears constantly throughout the description, at all levels, of Catholic life. It is the sense of disillusion and uncertainty. And the reason is always the same—it is the feeling of being out of touch, isolated, not trusted.

What is authority?

It is, in fact, a lack of unity, of *community*. And community means authority. If the community is not working as a community this means that authority is not functioning properly. This crisis in the life of the Church really *is* a crisis of authority, because authority is about the creation of community, and if the Church fails to be a community it fails to be Christian, and becomes no more than an obsolescent political and welfare organization—which is what many people think it is.

If we can say truly that there is a crisis of authority, and go on from there to wonder in what it consists and what can be done about it, we must have a clear idea of what is meant by authority.

Authority is not the same thing as power. The usual reaction to this statement is 'No, of course it isn't, authority in the Church means service.' But this comment shows just as deep a misunderstanding of authority as the assumption that authority is another word for power. Authority in the Church has the same function as authority anywhere else, and neither power nor service expresses its nature. They simply describe ways of exercising it.

Authority is a word with the same root as 'author' and 'authorship'. We realize this relationship when we talk about someone being 'an authority', meaning that we can take his opinion on this subject as true, because he either is, or is close to, the *source* of information on this subject. Authority here is not a matter of power or even of greater cleverness, but simply of being close to the source, to the 'author', of information. Christ spoke 'with authority' about human life because of his close relationship to the 'author' of human life, and his way of speaking showed the assurance and conviction that come from this closeness.

So authority is about a relationship to the 'author'. This applies to any subject, and 'subject' here means in practice a group of people who are interested in a matter, who come together because of this interest. They form a community, bound together by their common devotion to the task or study in hand. Their 'authority'—their relation to the *sources* or 'authors' of their subject—is what binds them together and also what defines or describes the *kind* of community they are. A scientific community, for instance, is defined by the common interest in science, and its authority is its sources of information, its organization for research, and the people best able to pursue and express the latest results of research. A political community is one whose bond consists in common allegiance to a common ideal expressed, perhaps, by a statement of party aims and made effective by people who can interpret this and put it into practice because that is what they are there for. They are 'in authority' so

B

as to relate the whole group to its source and mission and make the mission effective thereby. Without authority of this kind the group would disintegrate, cease to be a community.

Authority is the community's reference to its source. It is its self-explanation, both the sign of its nature and the means whereby it accomplishes the purpose for which it exists, as a community. This is true of any community. It is true of the Church, therefore. Authority in the Church is the means whereby the community realizes its relationship to Christ, its author. It is the way in which it explains to itself what it is, what it is for, and what it must do about it.

The way in which authority *works* varies from one kind of community to another. It doesn't have to have a governing aspect if, for instance, the purpose of the community is mainly study. In that case all the organization that is necessary is some means of keeping people in touch with work being done, and a computer could do that, at least in theory. But if the community is concerned with a wider area of living, then there have to be *people* to act as the signs of the ultimate source and purpose (as the Queen is supposed to do for the British national community), to preserve the 'shape' of the community, so that people continue to be aware what it is for, and also to arrange for the effective carrying out of the community's aims.

There are three main functions of authority which are inter-related. In the Church they mean, first, that there have to be people who are in some sense the symbol of Christ, as author of the Christian community. The heart of the community is the Eucharist, in which Christ's 'authorship' is not only recalled but renewed. Consequently the people chosen to preside at the eucharistic assembly naturally act as symbols of Christ, in this sense. This is why the arrangement of practical authority in the Church is likely to be connected with the function of presiding at the Eucharist, since this is what indicates the kind of community the Church is.

Authority has to be, also, a kind of 'outline' of the whole community, revealing to it what it is. The Church is 'founded on the apostles', its model is the apostolic group around Christ, which is repeated in the eucharistic assembly around its president, who represents Christ. And the apostolic task is to preach. This means not only actual proclamation to the unconverted but also the ever-renewed explanation to the community of its own nature, so that the community *as a whole* can carry out its commission to preach with confidence. Authority, here, refers the community to its source by *expressing* the relationship, in so many words.

The third way in which authority works is by making it possible for the community to carry out the work which its nature dictates, and this means formulating norms of behaviour, pointing out what needs to be done and indicating the best way to do it. It means governing, in fact, though the method of government may vary. It is this last function of authority that usually overshadows the others, so that it appears that it is *by* governing—that is, by exercising power —that authority in the Church carries out its function of teaching and of representing Christ. And the Christian notion of authority appears to be different from the secular one simply because, in the Church, power is to be exercised with love and mercy, in a spirit of service. But, merciful or not, power and government are functions of authority, not its nature. The question then needs to be asked: how is a specifically Christian authority exercised? And the answer is, it is exercised, in all three functions, with the purpose of keeping the Church true to its nature and mission *in whatever way best suits the particular historical circumstances in which it is living*.

So in one period, as in Augustine's time, authority works by close contact between the bishop and his small diocese, an intensely personal and sometimes stormy relationship that is needed to offset the ferocious but impersonal fervour of various kinds of gnostic heresy, and the pervasive influence of a decadent paganism in a decadent Empire. This tightly knit and highly emotional set-up strengthens the unstable Christian community and gives it the human quality lacking in the amorphous culture of the Empire.

In the dark ages the members of the expanding Church were mostly uneducated, half-savage tribes. They were unimpressed by the traditional structures of Roman law and culture, with their emphasis on order and reason. The hierarchical organization of the Church was patterned by this Roman tradition, and this pattern persisted and kept the unwieldy mass together. But it was not this, primarily, that was the authority for the half-converted tribes and their unreliable kings. It was the charismatic authority of saints that impressed them, referring them to Christ by showing them a power and a life greater than that of the old gods. It was the monastic traditions, both the fiery Celtic and the more sober Benedictine one, that symbolized the holiness of the Church, and taught, by word and example, the meaning of the whole Christian community. A reminder of this embodiment of authority in monastic life still remains in the mitre and crozier of an abbot, whose authority among the people was once as great as, or greater than, that of the bishop.

The ideal of Christendom, in which to be human was to be Christian, informed the middle ages. The Christian community was *the* community, it included every aspect of life. So authority in the Church expressed this by referring the whole of society to Christ as its author, in the only way possible at the time. In a feudal society subject to the king, it was this hierarchy of government that gave shape and meaning to the community. The Church, therefore, showed by a similar hierarchical form that all human society finds its apex in Christ its author. It showed what kind of thing the Church is, but showed it historically.

Later, when the Church was clearly not co-terminous with secular society, even in theory, the same sort of structure had a different purpose. It was the symbol of the kingdom of God, still intact, still faithful, still a sign of God's authority no matter what went on outside. But because it had learned its shape in a feudal society it continued to express the idea of God's kingdom, or authority, by means of an official structure still feudal in nature. This was not because feudalism seemed a specially good thing but because the Church's unity and unchanging chain of obedience were an effective protest against the world's unfaithfulness. It was a sign of continuity and loyalty that could ignore the adventures of nation-states in a turmoil of experiment and strife. So the feudal structure could seem the natural and permanent one for the Church, so much so that to suggest that authority could take on new forms can seem like suggesting that authority should be scrapped.

The present crisis of authority, then, is not a matter of people resenting authority as such. It has happened because people find that a form of authority (that is, of referring the community to its source) which worked well in the past simply doesn't work the same way any more. The language of community has changed, people don't think and feel about any kind of authority as they used to do, though the need for authority is as great as ever it was. So when those who represent authority in the Church try to exercise it in the old way, what they are doing doesn't mean what it used to mean. It no longer 'speaks' about Christ and his authorship, it seems to 'speak' an ancient language, referring to an interesting but dead culture. What is needed, then, is not reiteration of the old language of authority, but the development of a new one. It already exists, though undeveloped. It is usable and it is deeply Christian, but it is unfamiliar. It is so unfamiliar that it is sometimes hard to realize that it *is* a language of authority. It is this conflict between two notions of how authority works—the old, certain one, and the new, growing and still only semi-articulate one—that has created the crisis from which we are suffering.

I repeat: this is not a rebellion against authority, it is a search for an expression of it that is effective now. So to think of the crisis in terms of getting people to accept the old forms by modifying them and making them more humane and personal is not fully realistic and is doomed to disappointment. On the other hand it is equally unrealistic to suppose that the old forms can simply be removed, and a new start made. A new use of language emerges (sometimes very fast) from an older usage. However rapid the change it must be possible for the language *to continue to make sense* while it is changing. Otherwise there will be a total breakdown of communication and therefore of community.

This breakdown can happen *either* because the language of authority in the Church will not change, when the rest of the language of living is changing and leaving it behind, *or* because there are introduced new, experimental 'words' that have no roots in the past and therefore convey nothing except to a few 'with-it' experts. At the moment there seems to be a danger from both these causes, and the gap is widened more rapidly than the bridge can be built by those who are working —successfully—to assist the new 'language' to take shape. 'Crisis' is a scare word, but it is not unjustified in the circumstances.

What is the way forward? How can the Church rediscover itself under the newer forms, without losing its way and its wits in the meantime? There are parallels with earlier periods which, though not exact, are instructive. This epoch of the

Church displays some of the features of the age of Augustine, and also of the age of the barbarian conversions.

We live in a society that has a longish tradition of vast and stable government. The British Empire was not a purely British phenomenon, but was one particularly marked example of certain assumptions about government, the role of an élite, the supremacy of law and reason over emotion and 'art'. But this tradition is a past one; and we are left with the surviving structures, without the conviction and self-confidence that made them work. This situation is not unlike that of the late Roman Empire.

There are two separate kinds of culture at work at the same time. One is the cynical, disillusioned, anything-for-kicks, 'swinging' philosophy of life that is typical of a dying culture. Even material prosperity doesn't seem all that worth-while, though it is about the only thing one can be certain of, and inevitably sexual immorality of a hectic and depressing kind is common.

But curiously mixed with this (it shows chiefly among the young) are the signs of strong 'barbarian' culture. This is not new, it has been there a very long time, but so far always interpreted in terms of the other, ruling culture. And it shows itself chiefly amongst the young, because suddenly they have money and freedom; yet it is not essentially a phenomenon of youth but rather the outbreak, among the young, of a vivid and confident culture that we have hitherto either ignored or patronized. This culture lacks individual selfconsciousness and therefore identifies itself with its leaders, who emerge from the mass as its representatives and are followed devotedly and even hysterically. These heroes *are* their fol-lowers, in rather the same sense that the kings or chiefs of barbarian tribes actually *were* their people. People who live in this kind of culture are impervious to the law and order type of authority, not because they are immoral but because such

authority speaks a language that is, to them, quite meaningless. But they are very susceptible to charismatic leadership.

These two cultures are distinct, but they often overlap
in the same individuals, and produce a disturbing composite
culture that must surely be historically unique.

What form of authority in the Church can meet the needs
of both these interacting cultures? If the past is any guide, the
answer is not difficult to state, though very difficult to put
into practice.

One culture is pervasive, impersonal, isolating and hopeless. It expects no future and puts no value even on the
isolated experiences that give interest to the futile cycle of
human life. It affects even those who are in no obvious way
immoral or irresponsible. It robs people of a sense of purpose, either individual or communal, it makes them afraid to
commit themselves to anything but immediate aims, and
destroys satisfaction even in these. It denies mutual responsibility and the possibility of deep personal relationships, and uses the structures of society rather than being
part of them. In other words, it lacks authority that could
give a sense of the meaning of community.

The need here is for people to feel they belong together.
Authority in such circumstances needs to provide an opportunity for close and felt mutual responsibility and love. It
calls for a Christian community that is personal in feeling,
even emotional about itself and in its internal relationships,
but official, because that is a stabilizing and supporting thing.

The other culture is warm and lively and (by outside
standards) amoral. It rejects abstract or external moral
standards not so much out of defiance as out of a total lack of
comprehension of what they could be about. But it has its
own strong loyalties, its own code of behaviour which is
fiercely enforced. It can be violent and cruel but it is not cold
or cynical. If this were the only kind of culture it would prob-

ably work rather well, as the barbarian cultures of the dark ages worked, and left behind marvellous works of art. These cultures horrify us, but they could produce heroism, selfless courage, endurance and faithfulness to death, as well as sculpture, painting and literature far more living and moving than that of decadent Rome.

The same attitude to life can and does still produce these qualities, but at the moment it is engaged in a strife of mounting and mutual incomprehension with the forces of the older society. And the older society is undermined by its own lack of self-confidence. And out of all this come the writers and thinkers who try to express the ideals of the emerging barbarism, and find a political form that can articulate them without killing them. The new barbarians are not interested in left-wing poets and politicians, they aren't interested in poetry or politics at all, though the elements of both are the very shape of their living. But the poets and the politicians (I don't mean professional party ones, with exceptions) *are* interested in them and try to see what makes them tick.

If the Church is to be a community that matches the needs of this culture, it must understand in Christian terms what makes it tick. The signs of this are the devotion to its own heroes and heroines, the admiration for courage, the hatred of disloyalty to the group, the scorn for all that seems to be avoiding the realities of life. If the Church is to match this reckless vitality it must be visibly what it has been, and has never altogether ceased to be: a community capable of producing saints. It is real, personal, visible holiness that is needed. Authority here means the charismatic authority of the dedicated Christian. As it did in the dark ages, this kind of authority can work because it is framed by the continuing official structures of authority that ensure continuity and a sense of the overall reality of the Church beyond the scope of individual achievement, however great.

These two forms of authority are both needed, and together they make a pattern very different from the one we have been used to, but one that grows out of the past by a natural though rapid evolution.

What could this new pattern mean in practice, in terms of the immediate future of the Church? To see this it is necessary to look at what is already happening. The Church does not develop according to schemes drawn up by brilliant individuals or even committees, but by the apparently haphazard response of individual Christians, and groups of Christians, to immediate needs. The Spirit works through the whole Church and also outside its explicit membership, and it may be long before those who are sensitive to the breathing of God, and steer according to it, begin to realize that very many are moving in the same direction, blown by the same wind. But it is possible, at this stage, to see with some clarity the new directions of Christian development. The same things are happening in many parts of the world among people who have never met or heard of each other.

Two marks of the Christian today

There are two specially noticeable characteristics of Christian development at the moment, and they work in many different ways, according to varying circumstances. They show two aspects of Christian life which have always been there, but have varied in importance and have sometimes been obscured by other considerations.

One is a concern for the poor and unhappy. This has always been one of the marks of a true Christian life, but in the past it has generally taken the form of local efforts to relieve misery, either by individuals or groups. This is still necessary, and is still being done, but there is a new realization of the need to attack the conditions that breed misery, both at home and abroad. Even people who work at the immediate practical tasks are not content with them, but are often trying to make their efforts unnecessary by helping people to help themselves. And this includes making them politically conscious so that they will have sufficient confidence and hope to demand the reforms that are needed, and go on demanding until something is done. More and more, also, this effort to get at the causes of poverty drives people to the realization that the root cause of much of it is a totally corrupt economic and social system, based firmly (though often unadmittedly) on the incentive of private profit. The Pope's recent encyclical on world poverty expressed both this knowledge and the pressure of the sheer quantity of human misery that forces people to realize what is wrong and do something about it.

At an even deeper level the concern for the poor is part of a desire for poverty, a need to *be* poor, for the sake of the gospel. This has always been the desire of Christians who saw Christ most clearly, and in the past it has usually meant the profession of poverty, in religious life. What is new, and significant, is the spread of this need to be poor among lay people. At the same time there is a great deal of heart-searching among religious who realize that their poverty is often merely technical, that they enjoy a comfortable even though not luxurious life and absolute security, whereas 'worldly' people struggle with constant anxiety about money, and often enough with real privation. Some of the newer religious groups have arisen out of this compelling need to be *really* poor among the poor.

At all levels of the Church's life this vision of poverty is at work. The reduction of outward signs of authority among the bishops is a symptom of the same feeling, and some have gone further than others. A few have abandoned episcopal palaces to live among their people, have refused money to build churches because houses and hospitals are more needed.

This spirit of love for the poor and for poverty can be seen everywhere, but in the Church it can be named and recognized for what it truly is. It is the spirit of Christ whose poverty was total, and as Christian it expresses fully the less defined but equally urgent sense of responsibility for the poor that is evident in the whole of our society as never before. If the work of the Church is to show the world the real source in Christ of its half-understood hopes and fears, then here is a place where the charisma that the modern world needs is likely to appear. If authority is the way a community discovers its relation to its author, then the charisma that can show the world who is its author and its end is the blazing charity of people who are poor and love the poor, like Christ. This is a sign of authority that the new barbarians can recognize, because they are on that wavelength themselves much more readily than the privileged. Holiness is something anyone can recognize. Some may not want to and may hate it as a 'threat to their security', but more have been waiting all their lives for the least sign of it, never knowing what it was they seemed to be missing. And among the signs of holiness that are most intelligible to our time the love of the poor, to the extent of sharing their poverty, is pre-eminent.

The other recurring mark of the modern Christian effort is connected with this hunger for poverty, because it has to do with the same desire to abolish barriers and make genuine brotherly love immediate and effective. It is the new emphasis on community, and so much has been written about it from the theoretical angle that it would be a waste of time to add to it in the small space available in this book. Christianity is essentially about community, because the new life to which we are called is a shared, a common life. The Church is not a collection of individuals who are saved,

and who work out their salvation by loving and serving each
other. Rather salvation comes to them in the experience of
love and service, which is the life of the risen Christ in them.
This has always been true, but at times an individualist piety,
with the emphasis on detachment and the rejection of the
world, put this doctrine in the shade for a while.

(In fact, those Christians who were truly detached, who
really didn't care about possession or their own credit, or
about being understood or appreciated—they were people
with a huge capacity for real loving. But when their spon-
taneous rejection of things that interfered with whole-hearted
love of God and men was interpreted by others as a virtue to
be cultivated for its own sake the result could easily be a
travesty of what is meant by detachment.)

The interesting thing about the modern emphasis on community is that it is so widespread and so varied in the way it
is realized. The idea has been developed theologically in a
most exciting way, but the theology is shown in action, in
practice, among people who would scarcely recognize the
theology. It is in the dying-empire culture of our society,
which affects most of the West (even America, whose empire
is merely sick so far) that Christians who care most deeply
come together in smallish groups of all descriptions, to talk,
to share impressions and hopes, to pray and to plan their
work as Christians. In earlier times groups like these nearly
always formed a celibate religious community, or joined one,
but these new groups are mainly composed of lay people,
often with one or two priests among them, sometimes to take
a lead, sometimes simply to take part with the rest.

This change in the membership of such groups reflects another reason for the new desire for a clearer experience of
love in the Christian community. The development of the
theology of marriage has shown that the love of one human
being for another can be truly a saving thing, an experience

of God. And when the quality of married love as a Christian thing is fully recognized it poses a challenge to the Christian community: if this love is the love of Christ for the Church that means that it is the love by which that Church lives—or should live. Is there really *this* quality of love between the members of Christ? And if not, why not?

And it is in their efforts to realize this depth of charity in their community, and so bring it to a wider community, that such groups reach a point where their relationships seem to demand some action that expresses it more fully than discussion and planning and drinking coffee and even praying together can do. The love between a man and woman develops to a point at which it seems to require the consummation of a common life that includes full sexual union in order to express adequately what it really is. In the same way the development of a community as Christian reaches a point at which only the consummation of the relationship in the celebration of the Eucharist is an adequate expression of what is going on. This happens constantly, and sometimes it is possible for the desire to be fulfilled. The result of this is to make the community begin to spread out and expand its effectiveness, so that in some cases the original group breaks up in order to begin the work over again with new people. The purpose of a group of this kind is not primarily to comfort and support its members. It does do this, as a family does, but the support helps them to grow as family life should, so that they cease to care for their own comfort and want, instead, to give to others the love they have learned to share. On the other hand groups that do not go on to the celebration of the Eucharist often lack this dynamic quality.

Basically, it is this psychological fact about the experience of creating community that underlies the need for liturgical reform. Words like 'participation', 'priesthood of the laity' and so on are ways of expressing this need to create a real community and the realization that it can only be fully Christian if it finds its expression in the liturgy. And some of the worst frustration is suffered by clergy and laity alike when they know this and are denied the opportunity to celebrate and create their unity in Christ in a liturgy that really means what it says—visibly, simply and lovingly. The warmth and dynamic power of such a community are precisely what our society needs, and if such groups start small they do not remain self-enclosed. They are the leaven that could work through the whole lump of the Church. (Committees can never be the germ of new life, though they can be useful in pruning and training luxuriant growth. At present there is little growth for them to train.)

The bishop's place

Here, in these spontaneously arising groups, devoted to every kind of Christian work from the most theoretical study to the most immediately practical action, is a form of Christian life that can show people what the Church is. In a sense, then, it is a form of authority, or it could be, but it lacks the symbolic link that would show its connection with the Church at large, the whole people of God. This is what the bishop, and only the bishop, must be. And it seems that too often the bishop not only is not that link but refuses to see that there is anything there that needs such recognition and leadership. (One such community was built up over several years and was enormously rich in brotherly love, practical and effective charity. Its witness to Christ had brought many back to a lost faith, and converted others to it. The bishop sent an observer—to take note of every deviation of their liturgy from the exact current rubrics, and report back. The list was detailed, but the observer was too busy counting signs of the cross omitted to notice the one thing that struck everyone else—the overwhelming atmosphere of joy and love.)

Everybody criticizes bishops. It has become almost a new parlour game, swapping the latest story about bishops who are silly or funny or tyrannical or ignorant. Maybe they are all true. Maybe there are many other even more discreditable facts that are not known. Or maybe they are all lies. The point is not whether the criticisms are justified in detail, but why there is this immense discontent which all seems to focus on the bishops.

I think the reason is the Council. The debates that were reported, and the documents that resulted, were mixed, certainly, but on the whole they were of a quality that suddenly made it seem that bishops were not simply fatherly administrators, carrying out even more super-paternal directives from Rome. They were men of vision and determination, who would not be deterred from the total renewal of the Church. This may be a very unrealistic view, but it sprang from the immense need Christians felt for this kind of leadership. The new vision that the Council brought to the whole Church made people long for a leadership to match it, one such as the document on the Church itself envisages, and out of the greatness of the need grew a conviction that it must be forthcoming. This is very unfair on the bishops, who are not supermen and who have an exceedingly difficult job to do. But, unfair or not, people do feel let down, do find that 'no' is the usual answer to initiatives. Too often they are not led, but told to keep quiet until what they have to do has been decided from above.

The whole sense of disillusion, the protests—polite or not —the defections and the grumbles, all are aimed at the bishops or blamed on the bishops. Why? What is it that people really want from bishops and in many cases aren't getting? (In some places they do get it—it's sad how seldom people hear about that.)

What people want, because the Council taught them to, is something very impressive indeed, meeting the need of the time but firmly in the tradition of the apostles and of the Church through the centuries. It is the key to the renewal of the Church and the conversion of the world, because it is about real Christian authority, which alone can make a real Christian community.

Perhaps saying clearly what sort of bishop the people of God needs at this time may serve two purposes. It may crystallize vague discontent and substitute a good to be hoped for, even demanded, for rationalizations about not-really-expecting-bishops-to-be-much-help, which are probably the result of disappointment rather than realism. And also it may show the men who express authority in the Church—bishops, but also other clergy—that they are not just an Aunt Sally for everything that doesn't go right. Even the 'simple faithful' are not so simple that they expect the impossible and, if people expect a lot from bishops, that is realistic, according to the realism of the kingdom of God. It is *Christ's* authority that is being expressed, and if his people make great demands on their leaders this is a compliment, and an act of faith. (Admittedly it doesn't often sound like that.)

It is a good thing to be a bishop. Perhaps that needs saying at a time when it also needs saying, for instance, that it is a good thing to be a father. A father is a person who gives life, and that is what a bishop is for. Not alone, but with all the other people of God, in whom that life grows. A bishop is able to give life, that is what he is for, whatever kind of a person he is. But because he is *officially* a life-giver, a giver of Christ's life, he occupies a symbolic position that makes huge demands since, whether he likes it or not, he is being Christ in this role and will be judged accordingly.

What does this mean, now, in practice? A diocese is big, and contacts with individuals in given parishes are brief and infrequent. They tend, therefore, to be impersonal, as if that were a necessary result of the multiplication of small encounters. But a meeting need not be trivial because it is short. It may even be more effective, more life-bringing, because it is concentrated and unique in the life of each person encountered. Christ met thousands of people, some for only a few seconds, but they never forgot him because he loved each of them. It is never impossible to love.

And to love means to trust. This is probably the most important thing that people want, and seldom get, from their bishops. It emerges as the root cause of most of the present sickness in the Church, and finally of the crisis of authority itself. Lack of trust means lack of communication, waste of effort, discouragement, rebellion, even despair. What does it mean for a bishop to trust his people?

It means, first of all, that he trusts himself as their bishop. He is a man whose office is to bless, to give life. He is sent by the Spirit, he doesn't need to bolster up his authority with pomp and formality. A bishop should be able to trust himself and his office as Spirit-endowed, and get rid of the clutter of ceremony in dress and entourage that separates him from the people to whom he is sent. When he really trusts himself—which means trusting God—he can trust the people who work with him and for him. The Council's Decree on the office of bishops has a lot to say about this. When someone has an idea and wants to try something new the bishop will trust him to try and will advise if necessary, but not interfere. If it fails he will help him to overcome discouragement and try again. He will normally say 'yes' if he possibly can, and give clear reasons if he can't. He will ask for help and suggestions. He will consult the people concerned over every decision, and if possible let them make it.

If this real trust exists it will take certain concrete forms, to meet the needs of the time—a time in which community and mutual responsibility are the ideals of society. Democracy is not primarily important because it gives everyone a share in decision-making, but because as a *result of this* everyone feels involved in the decisions made. Once, the king was the personality of the people. His decisions *were* theirs, and they did feel involved. That is no longer so, therefore the need for people to be involved must be met some other way, and the only way available in our society is the democratic one. It isn't ideal, it is as open to abuse as any monarchy, and often messier, more unjust and more tyrannical. But it is all we have, *if* people are to feel involved. Democracy in the Church is needed for this reason. It solves nothing, in itself, but it can make people feel they are part of what is being done. At present they don't. So if bishops were elected, and had an elected advisory body to help them, it would not necessarily mean better bishops or more efficient administration, but it could mean that people would be more aware of who and what their bishop was (it's surprising how many don't even know who their bishop *is*) and more concerned about the affairs of the diocese. Whether and when that will come is impossible for a layman to guess; it is being done, bit by bit, in some places. But the reasons for wanting it are closely linked with the overriding need for trust between bishops and their people.

Connected with this, and one aspect of the need for trust, is the importance of some outlet that would enable conflict to be fruitful. Conflict of some kind there has to be if there is to be growth. It is not an accident that fervent Christian (and not only Christian) communities have usually found it neces- sary to provide for public expression of mutual criticism. If there is trust and love then even severe criticism can be ac- cepted, with humility and profit, between those under authority and those in authority, as well as between people of the same status. If there were elected assemblies of some kind at different levels of the Church they could serve this kind of purpose; but the important thing is the creation of an atmosphere in which criticism does not automatically appear as a threat. And although everyone has to contribute to this the bishop has to take the lead, or all other efforts are wasted.

It is the bishop who—without immediate drastic alteration of existing structures—can be the key-stone of the emerging forms of authority. Because people, now, need to be related to Christ in this way, his exercise of authority can be personal, direct, democratic, as informal as the occasion allows, clearly and undemandingly loving, and therefore absolutely trusting. Trust is one of the most difficult qualities to develop because it requires immense selflessness, courage, and faith. But without it the people of God will lack the leadership they need. When they get it, they respond.

The crisis of authority can be and must be the beginning of a new authority, one closer to the gospel, more human and more challenging to the ordinary Christian. Within the structure of official authority of this kind the charismatic power that is so evidently at work in the Church will have a chance to reveal itself fully. It will not challenge the authority that governs, though it may sometimes rebuke it, but it will fulfil its meaning. In this way the Church can be what it has to be for both the intermingled cultures of our society. Perhaps, too, the people who have so much feared the results of change might be led to recognize the work of the Spirit. Argument will never convince them, but love might.

Two

Cardinal Heenan

This part of the book has no calculated relevance to the preceding pages which, at the time of this writing, I have not read. My comment on what has gone before will be made in a later section. Here I propose to give a view, which may differ substantially from that of a layman, of what is happening in the Church. It is well to realize that nobody is entirely objective in making judgements. Even a judge is unlikely to approach a trial without bias if the facts of the case are already known to him. Because he is a professional it is, of course, easier for him than for a layman to put aside prejudice. It was a fictitious judge who made it his rule to dispense justice neither partial on the one hand nor impartial on the other.

Experience teaches us to be wary of our own as well as other people's protestations of objectivity. Few of us are able to rise above the influences of our home, early education and, above all, the fashions of thought in our generation. It is not therefore remarkable that young people are rarely different from each other. Despite appearances a characteristic of today's youth is its intense conformity. They may seem revolutionary but this is because revolution is in fashion. Advertisers—especially through television—make people want to possess the same goods and behave in the same way. Conformity has always been a characteristic of youth but the young people of our time are probably more conformist than their grandparents were in their day.

It is easy for an old man to see the folly of youth. With his failing sight it is more difficult for him to read at close range and recognize the stupidities of age. Most intelligent people are rebels and radicals in their late teens and early twenties. An adult probably cannot remember his own youthful foolishness nor recall precisely when he relinquished adolescent poses. The young through no fault of their own lack the experience which remedied the follies of their parents. Older people should acknowledge that the young behave more or less as they themselves once behaved. Opportunities for self-indulgence have been immeasurably extended because of higher living conditions and greater freedom of action. The more permissive attitude to behaviour has some bearing on the present conflict within the Church. A spirit of impatience with authority was set in motion by the Council. It is, perhaps, its most unfortunate by-product. But the gains from the Council are overwhelmingly greater than the incidental losses.

I thank God each day for Pope John and the Second Vatican Council. I believe that the Catholic Church might have entered a new dark age had not God's merciful providence given us the chance of reform. I further believe that the Church will emerge from the present post-conciliar trials strengthened and purified. We shall have to pay a price in the coin of suffering since pride can be brought low only by mortal wounds. In the Church there are two main strongholds of the proud. In one are those who refuse to admit that the Church had anything to learn from the Council. In the other are those who delight in dismaying their fellow Catholics by denying that anything at all was lovely in the pre-conciliar Church. Their motto is *Recedant vetera, nova sint omnia* ('let what is old disappear, let everything be new').

Before we forget what it looked like, we must attempt to recall the Church of the last decade. Let us not pretend that it was an evil institution. The word 'triumphalism' not yet having been coined, we did not feel it wrong to be proud of the Church of God. It is true that pride in family, nation or Church does not stand up well to analysis but there is no great harm in it. A man who claims to be English (German, Irish or American) 'and proud of it' rarely means exactly what he says. He probably means that he is grateful not to be a foreigner—for by definition a foreigner is someone alien, dissimilar, unattractive. Every man, in other words, loves his own people. He understands them because he is one of them. He forgives their misdeeds and takes pleasure (pride) in their victories and virtues. It is, of course, irrational to be proud of being born in Huddersfield, Yorkshire instead of Leigh, Lancashire. The Wars of the Roses were no less foolish than most other wars. When we talked of being proud to be Catholics we meant only that we were grateful for the gift of faith. Being Catholic, in fact, is a reason less for pride than humility. Even if we are converts we have no right to take pride in ourselves. Faith is God's gift, whether inherited or acquired by conversion. In neither case is it a credit to us personally. Pride in the faith, which need not connote triumphalism, is a recognition of the precious gift God made us in giving us the grace to be Catholics.

There is a right and wrong way of being proud. Before the Council we did not realize that there could be a wrong pride in being a Catholic. It is not wrong to be proud of our ancestry: 'Our fathers chained in prisons dark were still in heart and conscience free.' It is natural to take pride in those who distinguish themselves. Even winning an Olympic gold

medal or a first degree at a university gives joy to the
victor's family. Awards for physical courage give even greater
joy. No number of honours degrees is equal to one Victoria
Cross. This kind of pride animates English Catholics when
they think, for example, of St Thomas More. His moral
and physical courage made him the kind of man we all want
to become. The English martyrs are the chief source of our
pride in the faith.

There is, of course, much more than martyrdom to make us
proud. Most English Catholics, after all, have very scanty
knowledge of their martyrs. They know the story of the Protestant reformation in a very simplified version. What they
learned of history in school is remembered only in very broad
outline. To most Catholics the reformation means the lustful
and murderous King Henry VIII and the good pope who
refused him a divorce. The Catholic Church stood firm, the
story goes, preferring to lose England rather than compromise the law of God. This is thought to be not the whole
but the main story. It also happens to be the only version
which most English Catholics know. Their knowledge of the
papacy is also very limited. Gregory the Great is known
because it was he who sent St Augustine to convert the Angles
(whom he called angels). Nicholas Breakspeare is known (but
probably not by name) as the one English pope. A few have
also heard of Pio Nono, prisoner in the Vatican. Leo XIII,
although not likely to be familiar to the majority, is better
known than most popes because he wrote the encyclical
Rerum Novarum, called the Charter of the Workers.

All the popes of this century are with good reason esteemed
as holy men. Pope Pius X was the pope of the Eucharist who
suffered little children to come to Christ at the altar rails.
Benedict XV is vaguely remembered as the war-time pope
who effected the exchange of wounded prisoners. Pius XI
was the doughty pontiff who fought Mussolini, Hitler and

Stalin and wrote fierce encyclical letters condemning fascism, nazism and atheistic communism. Catholics in this country, having been brought up to fight for their faith and their schools, always admire a fighter. They had great affection for Pius XI.

Pope Pius XII was more widely known than any of his predecessors because during his pontificate increased speed of travel enabled more people to visit Rome. To tourists as well as pilgrims the Pope always made himself available. We now hear much about ecumenism but Pope Pius XII was a notable ecumenist before the word was current in Catholic circles. Protestant, Jew and Moslem were sure of a welcome at the Vatican. Pope Pius XII has been severely attacked in recent years for not protesting more vigorously against the Nazi persecution of the Jews. When all the documents are published his good name will be vindicated. It would have been easy for him to make strong protests from the safety of the Vatican. Courageous utterances are sometimes made by men who court popularity when it requires greater courage to keep quiet. Speeches against the persecutors of the Jews might have brought greater suffering to that unfortunate race which was the object of the hatred of a ruthless paranoiac. As soon as the war was over the Chief Rabbi of Rome became a Catholic. He knew what Pius XII had done quietly for the Jews. He must have been well satisfied with the Holy Father's record.

Then came Pope John. We must try to remember what the Church was like at the time of his death, which took place nearly three years before the end of the Council. To recapture the atmosphere of those days may help us to make a proper assessment of the post-conciliar Church. Belloc used to complain that people read history backwards. The same fault today is less euphoniously called hindsight. It is just as irrational to denounce the Catholics of yesterday for being old-fashioned as to laugh at Victorians. We would all have been smug Victorians had we not been born too late. It is unprofitable to criticize people for lacking ideas which became current only after their death. That is why we must try to recapture the climate in Pope John's pre-conciliar Church.

What was unthinkable even ten or twenty years ago we now take for granted. We used to be docile in accepting strict and even harmful regulations. Consider as an example the discipline in the sacramental life of priests and people. Think, in particular, of the eucharistic fast and the rules governing the celebration of Mass.

Until the liberalizing pontificate of Pope Pius XII Sunday could be a day of great trial for a young priest. His second Mass might be celebrated at eleven or twelve o'clock. His whole morning after the early Mass was spent in praying, preaching, hearing confessions and, perhaps, travelling. He had to do all this without even a glass of water. This unduly long fast did physical damage to some young priests. The rule of fasting from midnight was regarded as so sacred that only danger of death justified non-fasting Communion. During the second world war it was an event comparable with the victory of Stalingrad—or, better still, the retreat from Dunkirk—when the Holy See allowed priests working all night in an air raid to take a cup of tea before Mass. Some bishops fearing danger of irreverence towards the holy Eucharist did not promulgate the dispensation. It did not occur to priests to disobey. Discipline within the Catholic Church was the wonder and admiration of all outside.

Then Pope Pius XII introduced evening Mass. Since it now became impossible to retain the midnight rule, a fast of three hours was prescribed. Even this modified fast soon proved to be unsatisfactory. It was impossibly difficult for many people who had worked hard all day to fast for three hours in the evening. Bishops petitioned the Pope before the Council to reduce the fast to symbolic terms but Pope John thought this to be too revolutionary. It was not until the Council was half over that Pope Paul allowed Mass to be said at any time with the token fast of one hour. It is difficult now to recall the hardship imposed by the old eucharistic fast on frequent communicants.

We can learn a great deal from this example of the eucharistic fast. It illustrates, in the first place, the prompt unquestioning obedience of the whole Catholic world to Rome. We criticized the prelates who in the Roman Congregations decided which requests the Holy See would grant. We might have grumbled but we did not rebel. We gave no thought to revolt because the men who refused our requests were the representatives of the Holy Father. That was enough. No bishop, priest or layman would have been disloyal to the Vicar of Christ. His person, his words and even his lowliest representatives commanded our respect. We did not foresee the day when a priest would call the pope a liar. Such conceit and self-righteousness would have been quite simply beyond our imagination.

Universal loyalty to the pope was coupled with affection. Scarcely a Catholic home was without its picture of the Holy Father ('God bless our pope the great, the good'). This uncritical attitude could not be expected to survive the growth of communications. *Omne ignotum pro magnifico* ('the other side of the hill is always green') is generally true. Now that the pope appears on our television screens he has lost some of his magic. The Vicar of Christ has been regarded by Catholics as almost divine. They have paid filial regard to papal authority even when it has been delegated to others. This, in fact, is the rule. The pope's power is now exercised largely by the Roman Curia.

Through the Council the whole world came to know of the hostility of certain northern Europeans towards the Roman Curia. Its significance should not be exaggerated because it is their attitude towards all dictatorial authorities. It is impossible to interpret the motives of those who displayed an anti-Curia mentality during the Council without looking briefly at the social history of the first half of the twentieth century. It has been a formidable period for northern Europe. Ours has been the bloodiest century of all time. It has also been the century of man's greatest triumphs. The two are connected. Two world wars stimulated inventions which have given man his present astonishing power over the forces of nature. The European mainland was a battle-ground during the world wars. Some nations were twice overrun within the space of twenty-five years. Almost alone among the countries of Europe the British Isles have not experienced the horror of military invasion and alien rule. We have, of course, suffered in some measure. Our cities were bombed, both soldiers and civilians were killed in thousands. By comparison with the citizens of the continent, however, we have had little to endure.

Men and women who have lived in fear, liable to molestation by secret police, are marked for life. The outlook of northern Europeans on authoritarianism of every kind had much to do with their approach to the Council. Germans, French, Belgians and Dutch in different degrees experienced life under Hitler. This made them sensitive to any denial of liberty. They came to the Council determined to challenge the centralization of the Church which had given undue power to Italian prelates. They were not anti-papal but, in some sense, anti-Roman. They wanted to internationalize the Curia and, above all, to liberalize academic life within the Church. They knew that in John XXIII they had a pope who favoured what may be loosely called Christian humanism. (Pope John is merely caricatured, however, when he is described as consigning all rule books to the flames. To the end of his life he was a model seminary priest rarely departing from his own simple book of rules. This is clearly shown in his published diaries. His policy was to replace fear with trust.) The Church of Pope John would lovingly embrace all Christians and, indeed, all the children of God.

For half a century Catholic theologians had been accustomed to hold their peace, kept quiet by an over-protective and frightened mother. The Holy See in the early years of the twentieth century had lost nerve in face of a threat from within. Modernism, a serious danger to the Church, was made to appear even more dangerous by the clamour of its protagonists. They were assiduous writers, not above using half a dozen pseudonyms to give the impression of big battalions. Small wonder if bishops began to echo the cry of St Jerome who once exclaimed in anguish that the whole world had become Arian. The encyclical *Pascendi*, although welcomed by most Catholics, was responsible for the persecution of some genuine and devout scholars. Every interpretation of scripture not hallowed by tradition was condemned as modernistic. An oath against modernism was required of a candidate before each new step in his journey towards the priesthood, and when receiving an academic degree or taking ecclesiastical office. Modernism was, of course, dangerous and the sanctions applied by the Holy See were well intended. It is nevertheless clear to us now that the panic policy of the Church was responsible for the suppression of genuine scholarship. Pope Pius X was undoubtedly a saint but this does not prove that the methods used in his anti-modernist campaign were always right or wise.

The exuberant irresponsibility of some Catholic writing since the Council is in part a delayed reaction to this suppression of academic freedom at the time of the modernistic panic. Originally the danger of modernism was thought to lie in its approach to sacred scripture: if it were permissible to question the literal truth of historical references, doubt the hitherto accepted authorship of the pentateuch, the psalms or even the gospels, how could Christianity itself survive? In due time, however, the attack went beyond the scripture scholars. Soon Pope Pius X was denouncing modernism as the synthesis of all heresies. God alone knows if the ruthless campaign did indeed save the Church from the poison of error. It certainly emphasized the magisterium of the Church of Rome and aroused the undisguised envy of other religious bodies equally embarrassed by their own modernists but unable to silence them. It can be argued that the campaign, if not its methods, was providential. It is now obvious, however, that much needless pain was given to sincere and competent Catholic scholars—the wonder is that so few were driven out of the Church.

Not until the Second Vatican Council was half over did the Church rid herself of an exaggerated fear of modernism. It will be impossible to judge the full significance of the Second Vatican Council for many years to come. Almost all who took part in its controversies are still very much alive. The story of the Council was told to the world in the first place by secular journalists. They were not theologians or necessarily even believers. In writing their dispatches they relied on two main sources. The first was the meagre summary of speeches issued with apparent reluctance by the Vatican press office. Secondly, there were the interpretations of these handouts given in press conferences by theologians and clerical reporters. It was unfortunate that journalists from the very beginning divided bishops into liberals and conservatives, left and right, progressive and reactionary, as if they were writing about politicians. Few bishops earned or deserved their labels. Until the Acts of the Council are published the fact that the vast majority of the Fathers of the Council were open-minded cannot be established. All who were present know the truth. The same bishop might take a traditional line on one question and advocate radical change on another. Few approached all questions with prejudice.

It was tempting to picture meetings of the Council as if they had been outsize parliamentary debates. The Council, in fact, bore no more resemblance to the House of Commons than to the General Assembly of the United Nations. The speeches in the Commons or in the United Nations are almost always predictable. Each man is a partisan, that is, a party man. On only rare occasions in parliament is a free vote taken. Permission is then given for members to speak according to their private convictions without respect to party allegiance. In the Council every vote was a free vote. Each bishop who spoke in debate gave evidence of what he thought to be the faith of the clergy and faithful in his own diocese or nation. A few speakers, especially cardinals without dioceses, could give only their personal views. Their line of argument soon became predictable and for that reason their contributions were accorded little weight. It was usually necessary to await the speeches of bishops to discover what witness they would give. Voting was never according to party because there were no parties. Never according to nation because within most countries outlook differs according to geography. There are few countries in which there is no distinction, for example, between the views and temperament of citizens in the north and south. In Canada, U.S.A. and Latin America the racial and cultural divisions are marked and widespread. Even in European countries such as France and

Germany there were sharp contrasts of opinion. The press was never told this fact. French and German bishops were therefore journalistically labelled 'progressive'.

The debates in St Peter's, although not the most important feature of the Council, were the only public occasions. Commissions were far more important than the debates because it was their members who selected the material for debates. After the debates it was again the task of the commissions to sift the opinions of the Fathers and propose appropriate resolutions and amendments for suffrage. Commissioners were the key men of the Council.

Relatively few bishops spoke in the debates because speeches soon became repetitive and the closure was applied. The text of all speeches, whether delivered or not, was passed to the commissions. Some of the most effective speeches were never intended for delivery. It made little practical difference whether or not a man's voice was actually heard since his text was available to the commission. Archbishop Young of Hobart is an example of a bishop who rarely, if ever, spoke in debate yet made useful contributions to the Council. The minds of the bishops were nourished by lectures and discussions in the colleges where they lived or in one of the many halls put at their disposal during the years of the Council. Private conversations in small groups were often more effective than the debates in helping bishops to reach right conclusions.

The pastoral nature of the Council and the predominantly pastoral composition of its membership have not been sufficiently noted. More than a third of the Fathers were members of religious congregations. They were almost all missionaries who since ordination had been away from their monasteries. Of the other two-thirds many had become bishops after years as parish priests. Like the missionaries

these bishops had little acquaintance with the most recent
developments in scriptural exegesis and dogmatic theology.
They may be compared with general practitioners who keep
abreast of research by reading medical journals but have little
opportunity or inclination to read new text books. Most of
the remaining bishops had been raised to the episcopate after
years as teachers in colleges, seminaries or universities. Their
number was not small. It has been customary in some countries—Belgium and Ireland are examples—to recruit the
hierarchy largely from the staffs of seminaries. It is not
profitable to discuss which background best fits a man for
episcopal office. The Church needs both scholars and men of
practical experience. At the Council there were bishops with
the widest possible variety of qualification to witness to the
faith of their priests and people.

There are never enough bishops with up-to-date theological equipment to conduct the whole business of a Council
—not even of a pastoral Council. Professional theologians,
scripture scholars, philosophers, historians and canonists are
needed to ensure that the Fathers are well informed. At the
Second Vatican Council these men were described as *periti*
(experts). Without them the Council would have failed. The
names of most of them are unknown to the public but their
contribution to the Council was immense. In the Secretariat
for Promoting Christian Unity, of which I was a member,
there was a host of experts, but few had written popular
books and their names are therefore little known. But men
like Volk, Stakemeier, Thijssen, Feiner and Dumont were
well known to those inside the Council. Every commission
had a similar quota of scholars chosen from all over the world.
The hidden efforts of these men made it possible for the
Council to function. They were abreast of current theological
thought. The bishops turned to them for information and

c

guidance. They did not catch the eye of journalists because they rarely took part in the press conferences. These were the real stalwarts of the Council. Their labours made it possible for the bishops to reach near unanimity on almost every topic and to give practical expression to Pope John's dream. In addition to the official Council *periti* of whom many were theologians of international repute other priests were brought to Rome by their own bishops. Apart from being private *periti*, these priests would benefit from contact with famous theologians. From England, Frs C. Davis, R. Redmond and T. Worden each came to one session of the Council at the invitation of the hierarchy.

Although the Council is still recent certain myths have already been widely accepted. These will not be discounted in our day because in all good faith journalists have spread them throughout the world. The more or less uniform version of the Second Vatican Council given by the press will hold the field until corrected by the historians of tomorrow, who will know even more about the Council than those who took part. This is not surprising. In the twentieth century we know far more about the scriptures than the Christians of eighteen hundred years ago.

The chief myth of the Council is that a small group of avant-garde *periti* scored a brilliant victory over a vast mass of reactionary bishops. Another version of the myth is that the majority of the Council Fathers was composed of forward-looking prelates who had to fight continually against the machinations of a reactionary old guard. This myth was allowed to grow chiefly because until near the end of the Council the press was handled incompetently by the Vatican. During the Vatican Council of 1870 the dateline of a dispatch mattered little. At the Second Vatican Council the Holy See evidently thought that the demands of journalists had not changed in a hundred years. It did not realize that the press of today puts speed before most other considerations. One newspaper regards news as dead once it has been published by another. Since the official spokesmen were so slow, journalists had no option but to seek information elsewhere. There were not lacking theologians with 'inside information' who could make each debate sound like a fresh action in the battle against reaction. The good name of the Council was threatened by these clerical rumour-mongers.

Another myth is that the Council Fathers were bitterly divided. Every bishop in the world knows this to be untrue. In four years there were not half a dozen serious clashes and these did no harm to fraternal charity. Even when some of us made provocative speeches or used dramatic phrases to denounce documents offered for our approval there was rarely any show of anger. An impassioned speech was as likely to attract laughter as applause. The Council was the best tempered assembly imaginable. Little as the bishops relished prolonged absence from their dioceses they were genuinely sad at the end of the Council when it came to the parting of friends. The friendships formed at the Council are proving valuable now. Exchange of views and visits is helping bishops in many lands to solve their pastoral problems. I doubt if words like 'conservative' or 'progressive' figure much in their conversations. The unity among Catholic bishops despite their racial and cultural differences is little short of miraculous.

We are still in the early days of the post-conciliar Church. So far only a few decrees have been given any great attention. One reason for this is that the documents of the Council are of uneven value. If we compare, for example, the document on mass media with the Constitution on the Church it is hard to credit that they were produced by the same Council. It is clear that the clergy who drew up the document on modern means of communications had been given a task beyond their powers. The Constitution on the Church, on the other hand, is competently composed and, in its final form, quite magnificent. The notice taken of other conciliar documents has depended largely on their popular appeal. The Statement on Religious Freedom, for example, has been much discussed. Catholics can quote it to applause in any company as proof of the new liberalizing spirit in the Church. In one sense it was a crucial document. Some contended that it represented a change of doctrine—although Pope John had warned the bishops at the opening of the Council not to contemplate any new dogmatic definitions. The Statement on Religious Freedom called for freedom of religious practice for the persecuted. It also indicated the need for a change of policy in certain countries where a Catholic majority might restrict the religious freedom of the rest. The debate was among the most lively of the Council. It was also perhaps the most misunderstood. Those who opposed the original wording of the Statement were too easily condemned as enemies of freedom. Their objections, however, concerned not freedom but truth. In its early versions the Statement could have been interpreted to mean that liberty of speech is sacrosanct and therefore in no circumstances must it yield to the claims of objective truth. As a result of the heated debates the final form is incomparably better than the first version which we of the Secretariat for Christian Unity offered to the Fathers. The right of men to follow their consciences even if in the Church's view their consciences are ill-informed is clearly laid down. It is well known that in certain countries intolerance has been practised by Catholics. The Council condemned this no less strongly than the intolerance of other religious bodies and of militant atheists. There still exist in the world crusading sects determined to destroy Christians wherever they are to be found.

A decree of which little has so far been heard deals with the missionary activity of the Church. It would be interesting to know why this important document has received such sparse comment. It may be that the whole idea of conversion has become distasteful. There has been a certain selectivity about the emphasis given to the various decisions of the Council. Inferior documents like the Statement on Education have been largely ignored for the good reason that they had nothing new to say. Recent popes in their encyclicals had already pronounced far more eloquently on the subject of Christian education. But the decree on missionary activity is clearly of fundamental importance in a missionary Church. The debate on the missions was, in fact, memorable because few who spoke were without missionary experience. It was exhilarating to listen to the earnest pleading of men bowed with years of labour in the mission fields. The onslaught on the first draft of the decree was devastating. Zeal for souls sharpened the eloquence of bishops from Africa and Asia who appealed for its total rejection.

The draft was eventually withdrawn and a much nobler decree emerged. The Council clearly laid down the duty of every member of the Church to be missionary-minded. Bishops in Europe and the new world must acknowledge henceforward their responsibility for the Church of the missions. Clergy in established parishes at home are told not only to collect funds but to offer themselves for active service in the mission field. The decree states simply that the very fact of being Christians means being missionaries. Laymen therefore are also called to volunteer to join the missionaries if their domestic duties permit. One result of the comparative silence about this decree is that an unbalanced view of the Council has been given to the Church and the world. It is whispered that the Church is no longer interested in spreading the word of God. Some of the more thought-

less have attacked the whole idea of conversion on the
grounds of its being an invasion of religious freedom. This is
a very far cry from Christ's command to preach the gospel
to every creature. It is forgotten that the first Christians were
all convert Jews.

This is a suitable point to consider certain views which
have gained currency since the Council although they do not
derive from the Council. Because they have gained currency
only since the Council they are thought by some young
priests and lay theologians to be part of its teaching. Not for
some years will it be possible to disentangle the various influences which have led to the outbreak of a kind of theological class war in the Church. The Council provided the
occasion, but was not the cause, of the establishment of a
theological school which has within it a potential for either
anarchy or enlightenment.

Those engaged in academic pursuits are naturally the most
affected by the views of modern theologians. They have the
opportunity of reading the new books which now proliferate.
Most other people have to be content with reading reviews
and articles.

The English are at a great disadvantage in the modern
theological world. We have had no theologian with original
ideas since Newman. Present religious writers—and this is
true also of the U.S.A.—merely transmit the views of continental theologians of whom the most prolific is the German
Jesuit, Karl Rahner, some of whose books are published
under joint authorship. His range is phenomenal—dogma,
pastoral theology, scripture, moral theology, philosophy and
liturgy; he is probably the outstanding theologian of our
time. His bold and imaginative writing is orthodox although
his style is so involved that even Germans often find the
original texts quite baffling.

It is unfair to serious theologians like Fr Rahner to describe their teaching as new theology. If it were entirely new it would be quite unacceptable to the Catholic Church. But for every Karl Rahner, there are ten lesser theologians, who do produce a new theology; many of their ideas come from northern Europe, and some of them are indeed difficult to reconcile with the teaching of God's Church. This is a pity not only because it misleads young people who instinctively seize on new ideas but also because it invites condemnation by the Church. We are still recovering from the effects of modernism and the reaction it produced. A similar reaction against what is already being described as neo-modernism could neutralize the liberalizing influence of the Second Vatican Council. We may not have another *Lamentabili* nor *Pascendi* nor another *Syllabus of Errors*, but the suppression of books could come again, to the dismay of lovers of the Church. Should this happen it will be the fault not of the Church but of the semi-skilled theologians who warp the minds of the young. Prayer, study and humility are essential to theologians if they are to bring their fellow Christians nearer to God.

Teilhard de Chardin was one of the victims of the anti-modernist campaign. Today he is regarded as prophet or heretic, according to taste. One suspects that fewer have read him than have read about him. Anyone can enjoy *Le Milieu Divin* but it requires formidable endurance to persevere to the end of *The Phenomenon of Man*. Chardin is a popular figure today partly, I think, because he is regarded as a victim of intolerance. Had he been allowed to write and publish freely his name might, indeed, be less often heard today but some of his ideas might have become part of our Catholic culture. Fr Teilhard was a saintly priest. He did not rebel or refrain from his pastoral ministrations when he fell victim to the anti-modernist purge. In this he was like most of the

scholars who suffered persecution. They remained faithful
to their prayers and therefore to the faith.

Teilhard was a man of prayer. That is how he learned to
obey. He listened to the voice of God rather than the voice of
men who urged him to defy his Jesuit superiors. When
modern Catholic writers provoke sanctions they are not always so humble. An entirely new notion of obedience has
arisen since the Council, and this has greatly damaged the
spiritual lives of some religious communities. It is forgotten
that when theological writing endangers the faith the Church
is under an obligation to take action; the indiscriminate publication of unorthodox theology forces the Church's hand.
It is much to be hoped that her hand will not be forced again.

It is impossible to discuss or understand the conflicts within the Church in the English-speaking world without con-
sidering what has been happening in recent years on the
continent of Europe. I have said that since Newman we have
had no great theologian. The reason is a very simple one.
England has had no Catholic nursery for theologians. Newman, after all, learned most of his theology at Oxford before
his conversion. One day Catholic students may once again
study theology at English universities. The growing co-
operation between theologians of every denomination makes
this increasingly likely. For many years a Catholic priest has
lectured in the theological faculty of Birmingham University.
It seems likely that Catholic theologians will eventually be
offered posts in all universities with a theological faculty.
Catholic seminaries, including Heythrop, the newly formed
athenaeum for philosophy and theology, already welcome
visiting non-Catholic lecturers. Meanwhile all English seminaries are seeking closer contact with the universities. Until
recently higher studies in theology had to be made abroad. In
consequence most theological publications in English are

little more than vernacular versions of theories current on the continent. That is another reason why it is difficult to diagnose the comparatively mild disorders within the Church at home without looking a little more closely at the Church abroad.

It would be foolish as well as impertinent for an English bishop to offer criticism of the Church in other countries. We have been called by God to keep our own house in order not to tell others what is wrong in theirs. Everyone now talks of the alleged turmoil in the Catholic Church in Holland. Many of the stories have come from the Dutch who live abroad and return home for holidays. Cardinal Alfrink, the Primate of Holland, denies that his flock is notably different from the rest of the Catholic world. He contends that the Dutch merely speak openly of matters which Catholics elsewhere discuss in secret. It is doubtless true that given any encouragement many young Catholics in other lands would be ready to follow the Dutch pattern. What is almost always forgotten by those who deplore the activities of Dutch Catholics is that religious unrest is only part of a general pattern in Dutch society. It was Holland which produced the young 'Provos' determined to revolutionize the outlook of the whole country. It is difficult for foreigners to know what significance should be attached to this movement: it may be a passing phase of youthful anarchy, it may be the cradle of a great social or political movement. Whatever it may be it is the product of history and as such deserves attention. Meanwhile the Catholic churches in Holland are crowded and the altar rails are filled. The fervour of this great Christian people has not suddenly evaporated.

Apart from the Poles, the war produced no more resourceful enemy of Hitler than the Dutch. Holland mobilized its resistance to the invader with the fury of fraternal hate and

with teutonic method. Before the second world war Holland
had been a religiously divided country. There had been tentative advances towards Christian Unity but apart from enthusiastic ecumenists most ordinary Protestants and Catholics mixed little more than the ancient Jews and Samaritans.
United against the invaders, however, the Christians of
Holland eagerly went to each other's aid and, to their great
credit, joined forces to protect many unfortunate Jews from
deportation and certain death. This small but disciplined
nation went to war in the only way open to it. Its meagre
troops had been overcome in a matter of hours and their
weapons captured. So it was left to the civilians to declare
war on the occupying army. When a child was old enough to
understand he was trained in sabotage. All citizens were
pledged to lie, cheat, steal, destroy and, in general, to harass
the enemy in every conceivable way. They came near to
breaking the hearts of their German oppressors. The resistance of the armed forces was pitifully inadequate but, according to most reports, the civilians were magnificent.

It was not until after the war that the Dutch people
realized the price they had paid for their glorious effort. It
was easy to teach a child to point north instead of south when
asked by a Nazi the way from Amsterdam to Rotterdam. Any
normal boy would be enchanted to receive permission to
steal or set fire to unguarded property. The day of reckoning
came when there was no longer any Nazi to lie to and no
German property to destroy. Habits of lying, cheating and
stealing are not easily broken. When the war was over the
anxious Dutch authorities had to devise a plan for the re-
education of youth. The churches, schools and cinemas combined to give each of the ten commandments in turn an air-
ing. For one week sermons, lessons, plays and films would
have a common theme—'thou shalt not steal' or 'thou shalt
not bear false witness'. In regarding the present restlessness

we must remember that the children of wartime Holland are the young and middle-aged men and women of today. They and their children may well be suffering still in some measure from the laudable anarchy of former days. It is important to realize that the problem is not exclusively religious. The royal family and the government in Holland have probably suffered as much as the Church from the current attitude to authority. This fact must be set against the stories of religious chaos coming out of the Netherlands to fill the press of England, France and the United States of America.

The press gives the impression that on the continent the whole community of clergy and laity is enthusiastically putting into operation the decrees of the Council. English Catholics must be forgiven if they picture a Europe ablaze with zeal for reform. In order better to judge the English scene it will repay us to look at other areas of the Church abroad. The Church in Germany holds a national Catholic lay congress every two years. It is called a Katholikentag. The last congress was held in 1966 in Bamberg. The object of the congress was to give leaders of lay organizations the opportunity of studying the decrees of the Vatican Council as they apply to the laity. This congress was of impressive size. There were over two thousand diocesan representatives and at the pastoral conference held in conjunction with the main convention five hundred priests were present. At the end of the conference visitors were allowed and the closing ceremonies attracted no less than thirty thousand people. It is worth noting that at Stuttgart two years previously the closing ceremonies attracted two hundred thousand of the faithful. But this fall in numbers may not be significant since Stuttgart is much more accessible than Bamberg. Nevertheless in view of the vast numbers of Catholics in Germany we may suspect that enthusiasm among the conference-going laity is not on the increase.

According to German reports of the Katholikentag—which may be inaccurate or exaggerated—the conference was greatly hampered because most of the laity were disposed to discuss religious problems mainly in terms of private devotion. These German Catholics are said to have been more concerned with their own spiritual lives than with the theological questions which were the chief interest of those who had organized the conference. Discussions were confused by arbitrary interpretation of conciliar texts. Most of those taking part in the conference apparently had not read the Council documents but were relying on commentaries written by popular theologians. There was uncertainty about what the Council had really intended. They felt it unwise to dismantle existing organizations before knowing more precisely what the Council was alleged to have wanted to put in their place. The majority at the conference were, of course, active members of Catholic organizations and were not reassured even when the organizers insisted that although out for reform they had no intention of dissolving existing Catholic societies. The Katholikentag is reported to have led to sharper suspicion and a greater cleavage between the innovators and the diocesan representatives of the laity.

This became most clear when the question of Catholic schools was under discussion. The overwhelming majority of those present were much in favour of denominational schools and opposed the idea of community schools for Catholic and Protestant children in the same locality. They feared that a Catholic pupil exposed to a non-Catholic teacher of history, for example, might have his faith disturbed.

The spirit of the Second Vatican Council is much talked of in Germany. It is understood that this new spirit imposes a sense of responsibility for the whole Church of God and for the world itself. It is well known how generously Catholics of Germany have interpreted their obligation towards the rest of the Catholic Church. Their great charitable organization Misereor is blessed in the arid Asian countryside and the impoverished villages of Africa and South America. There is much talk in Germany of the obligations of Catholics towards their fellow citizens. They are urged to honour the God-given rights of all and to respect not only other people's religious faith but even other people's unbelief. The German Catholic is exhorted to champion the welfare of society as a whole. He must think of Protestants and unbelievers as well as of his Catholic brethren. All these questions are dealt with extensively in lectures, books and journals but a German reporter wrote that 'these noble ideas are conspicuous by their total absence from the thoughts and lives of most German Catholics'. German Catholics, nevertheless, are interested in charitable works and amazingly generous to the needy in missionary lands. But the higher flights of post-conciliar sociological theory have not yet been grasped by most of the faithful. At the close of the Katholikentag the press pronounced its verdict. 'The predominant impression', wrote a leading German daily, 'is one of contradiction, opposition and unanswered questions. The effort to bring the Council into Germany is still standing at the starting line.'

The German hierarchy took note of the theological unrest in their country. They expressed regret that certain developments in recent theology had shaken the faith of many Catholics. They deplored the fact that even belief in God had become the subject of attack by brash theologians. They took approving note of the new and astonishing interest in theology among educated laity but warned amateur theologians that popular writing is often either incorrect or too sketchy to give readers a firm grasp of theological truth.

At the conclusion of their meeting the bishops issued a joint pastoral letter. This was received with enthusiasm by most German Catholics but had a scornful reception from the critics. These confessed their astonishment that this pastoral letter could have been written by the same episcopate which had been in the forefront of the 'progressive phalanx' at the Vatican Council. The pastoral letter said that the Church had entered a new chapter in its evolution. This is the phase of accepting and implementing the Council. It warned the clergy and faithful that the bishops will resolutely oppose misinterpretation of the Council and the 'cheapening and misuse of conciliar statements'. They were not at all happy about the state of the Church in Germany. What had been described at Bamberg as the healthy unrest arising from the Council now appeared to the bishops as unhealthy, confusing and misleading. They said that all scientific study and dialogue, like every other activity in the Church, must be guided by the principles of the faith. They condemned as enemies of true reform both those who inflexibly cling to the past and those who refuse to acknowledge that anything in the past was good.

Before making a closer examination of the conflicts within the Church in England let us glance also at the Church in Austria. This may further help us to guage our own relative progress. The number of people actively practising any religion in Austria is said to be regrettably small. But the Catholic community is influential and its opponents are largely anti-clericals. The Austrian hierarchy published a Letter to Priests early in 1967. From this it appears that the Church in Austria is in some ways even more troubled by divisions than the Church in Germany. The Austrian bishops are disturbed by the modern errors which imperil the faith of their people. They are particularly concerned about the attack on biblical truth ('here begins our real worry'). They are alarmed by what their people may have seen and heard on the radio and television. They make clear their disapproval of certain new approaches to the bible. They are particularly anxious to warn their people against the excessive demythologization associated with the Protestant theologian Bultmann.

Having warned their flock against certain features of recent biblical criticism (making reference to the writings of the Anglican Bishop of Woolwich) the bishops deal with recent attacks on the Eucharist. It appears that many educated Catholics had taken part in a holiday course of theology during the summer and had come back alarmed by what they had heard. Some of the lecturers had advanced extraordinary views about the real presence. We have heard echoes here of this iconoclastic thinking, but in England the exponents of false thinking on the Eucharist have been so few that the bishops have not found it necessary to make any official pronouncement on the subject. In Austria, apparently, great harm has been done by the foolish talk of some theologians. The bishops say:

> 'You have come back from last summer's courses with great fear because here and there it was said that the priest possesses the power to consecrate only when a community is present and that he acts on orders from a community. That after the celebration of Mass there is no longer an eucharistic presence. We well understand your worry. We share it with you and we must make an express declaration. These notions are clearly heretical. In the first place, according to the universal conviction of the Church's faith, the Holy Mass is at the same time a sacrifice and a communion. The first aspect cannot be passed over in silence.'

In Austria, as elsewhere, reformers have attempted to make the sacrifice of the Mass sound like a Protestant communion service. This, of course, is false ecumenism. Protestants in fact prefer to hear plain Catholic teaching rather than a slanted version.

The bishops condemn priests who refrain from offering daily Mass in defiance of the teaching of the Council and the encyclical on the Eucharist. The bishops conclude the passage on the Eucharist with these words:

'Just as we were especially concerned with the point about the bible because it deals with the foundation of our faith so we are concerned with the Mass because it is the cornerstone of our renewal. We therefore beg those brethren who have become uncertain in this matter to hearken to our words spoken with the consciousness of our grave responsibility.'

The Austrian bishops then talk of the authority of the hierarchy. They say:

'It is loudly proclaimed that there no longer exists a hierarchical Church. Let us examine, still in the light of the conciliar decrees, what is the persuasion of the Church's faith.'

The bishops quote various parts of the decrees of the Council which safeguard authority within the Church and remind the priests that they have no right whatever to alter anything in the liturgy 'therefore it is absolutely unlawful for anyone else even if he be a priest, to add to, to take away or to change at pleasure anything in the liturgy' (*Constitution on the Liturgy, 22*). The bishops continue:

'The intrinsic reason for this rule is that every arbitrary action constitutes a transgression against charity towards the community inasmuch as its communal character is disturbed. Therefore there is no doubt, according to the Council, that the order authorized in holy places is of such high value as to exclude every arbitrary change. In this the conscience of the faithful is on the side of the Council. "A house which is divided against itself is brought to desolation" (Matt. xii, 25). This disquietude, which has seized the faithful people, is certainly known to you. We are then responsible for seeing that the progress desired by the Council be genuine and does not overstep the limits assigned to it. Above all in your sermons explain the inner meaning of reform so that the faithful may follow it willingly and with joy.'

What do Catholics in England think about the post-conciliar Church? It is as difficult to answer that question as to say what the man-in-the-street is thinking. Our separated brethren talk of the man-in-the-street as the man-in-the-pew. Adopting their terminology, the man-in-the-pew for our purpose is presumably the practising Catholic. The answer is that even among practising Catholics there is considerable divergence of opinion. Many Catholics regard the Council as the greatest grace of their life after the faith itself. They rejoice at the new outlook of the Church and are exhilarated by the opportunities now confronting modern apostles. They unreservedly thank God that they have lived to see the aggiornamento.

They delight in the liturgical changes which have made the Mass more obviously a joint action in which priest and people participate. They had always longed to take a more active part in the liturgy and, before the Council, they unreservedly welcomed the Latin dialogue Mass. No longer was the Mass an isolated performance with the priest as actor or soloist and themselves as a passive audience. Before the Council they had

heard little of the priesthood of the laity. They readily accepted the notion and now rejoice that it is becoming a more
obvious reality. They feel themselves to be part of a worshipping community with a responsible role in the whole work
of salvation. They grasp the significance of the liturgy as a
continuous offering of prayer and action. They no longer regard the Mass as a mere ceremony with little relevance to the
other activities of their day. They appreciate more fully that
all the thoughts, words and actions of the day are offered to
God in the Holy Mass. They had always repeated this pious
phrase in their morning offering, but now relish it as the
theological expression of union in Christ. They understand
better what our Lord meant when he told his disciples 'that
they ought always to pray' (Luke xviii, 1).

These men and women who thank God for the Council
welcome the opportunity of a closer share in the whole work
of the Church. They are especially glad that responsibility
will no longer rest only on the shoulders of the clergy. Some
had resented what they took—usually wrongly—to be the
paternalism of the ordained minister. They feel that they
now have official sanction for assuming duties for which they
had always regarded themselves as better qualified than their
priests. From the documents of the Council they have seen
that the Church did not speak with different voices to the
clergy and laity. The decrees on the Lay Apostolate and on
the Priestly Ministry and Life use exactly the same language
and teach the same lessons. Both decrees make it clear that
the laity are to be not only allowed but positively encouraged
to take an initiative in apostolic work.

Zealous Catholics have always been active in various organizations. In every parish some men and women were, in
the old phrase, 'pillars of the Church'. They were ready to
undertake works of charity and spiritual enterprises of every
kind. But hitherto the faithful have worked not, so to speak,

as apostles in their own right but rather as lay assistants of the clergy. They have been told what to do and when to do it. If they took initiatives without awaiting orders from the priest they were in danger of being called anti-clericals. Anti-clericalism is a term almost always wrongly used in English-speaking lands. The average layman in dispute with his priest has usually fallen out because he thinks the priest is not sufficiently zealous or efficient. Your true anti-clerical opposes only the zealous and efficient clergy. He is anti-clerical because he is anti-God.

Other equally devout Catholics are inclined, on the whole, to deplore the changes brought about by the Vatican Council. For them the Council is a cross if not an actual disaster. There is little in the changes which appeals to them as beneficial to the salvation of souls. Even the use of the mother tongue in the Mass is regarded by some as a surrender to the spirit of the world. The converts among them are especially anguished because for them the loss of the Latin Mass appears as an attack on the unity of the world-wide Church. Longing for the familiar sounds and actions they now go joylessly to Mass. It was to be expected that some older people would be reluctant to break the devotional habits of a lifetime but their complaints are much more than the typical reaction of age to change. They loved the beauty of the Latin liturgy and are outraged by the sometimes unattractive translations and, above all, by the frequent experiments to which their Mass is being subjected.

For them the Mass had been the one stable feature in an ever-changing world. They sometimes mistakenly believe that the main motive for introducing the mother tongue was to effect a compromise pleasing to the separated brethren. Any liturgical innovation which makes the outward forms of the Mass more like Anglican worship they hold to be a betrayal. They look with suspicion on laymen who in their view are usurping priestly prerogatives. It brings them no comfort to see their fellow parishioners entering the sanctuary to read prayers and biblical texts during Mass. Nor do they relish the prospect of the administration of the parish by their fellow laity. They are ready to do whatever the priest asks but are not at all willing to be directed by other laymen.

The clergy, on the whole, are enthusiastic about the lay apostolate. They may be sceptical about what will happen if the laity take complete control of the material side of the parish but, obedient to the Council, they will allow their people to undertake real responsibility. They are prepared to erect Parish Councils and listen to the voice of the people's elected representatives. But they realize that much has to be learned before the schemes proposed by the Council will run smoothly in the parishes. At clerical fraternals Anglicans sometimes gently mock them with harrowing descriptions of their own Parish Councils. Lay-ridden parsons profess themselves amazed that their Roman Catholic colleagues should so innocently surrender their independence of lay control. Church wardens and Parish Councils protected by the rules of the Established Church sometimes make life difficult for incumbents. Nevertheless most priests are eager to carry out the recommendations of the Council. They hope that if all is done in the spirit of the Council fuller partnership with the laity will bring new strength to the spiritual and social life of the Church.

The object of our excursion to the post-conciliar Church abroad was to enable us to see our own position in better perspective. In England, as in most countries, a minority is impatient of all delay in putting into practice the decrees of the Council. Impatience does not normally foster unity and it would be wrong to pretend that there are no divisions within the Catholic community in England. Better to admit the existence of conflict and examine its causes. It is easy and, perhaps, natural to blame the clergy and especially the hierarchy when anything is wrong in the Church. It is also easy but equally unprofitable for clergy and bishops to blame the laity. Disputes in fact do not greatly matter if those in conflict are honestly seeking the good of the Church and of the whole community. The comforting fact is that most of the laity who criticize the hierarchy are in earnest. They sincerely believe that they are acting for the good of souls. Leaving aside those who have no love for the Church as an institution let us try to see to what extent the critics are right.

It is notoriously hard to distinguish between a man and his office. Critics are often wrong when they believe themselves to be inspired only by high motives in attacking those in authority. More often than most of us realize, our motives are mixed. The ferment in the Church—a ferment largely confined to that part of the Church which really cares about the Council—may be good or bad. It depends on what comes out of the ferment. Unrest in itself is neutral. Sometimes it is healthy, sometimes destructive. Quite certainly the present unrest has caused confusion among the rank and file of the Church. Most Catholics long for the peaceful days when as Catholics they had to withstand onslaughts only from enemies of the Church. They find it most uncongenial to defend the Church against their fellow Catholics.

Contemporary theology is not new. Genuine theologians are not producing new doctrine or denying the old. They are seeking to present the teaching of Christ in a fashion and in language which people of today can understand. Newman pointed out in his *Development of Doctrine* that within the deposit of faith the germs of every Catholic doctrine however recently defined are to be found. The Immaculate Conception is an example. You will search the scriptures in vain for its definition. It is enough that guided by the Holy Spirit the Church could find in holy scripture some warrant for belief that the soul of the Mother of God was full of grace from the moment of her conception.

'A naive credulity in scholarship gives many the false idea that salvation comes from scholarship. Our confrères occupied with the study of theology will agree with us when we point out that the Church was founded on the apostles and not on scholars. At the same time we well recognize the enormous problems committed to theology, especially today; we confidently entrust their solution and clarification to our professors' (Pastoral of the German bishops).

One distressing aspect of the unrest within the Church is persistent attack on the hierarchy by small groups. It is distressing not only because it hampers the pastoral work of the shepherds of the flock but also because it could become a major obstacle to reform. If bishops were forced to spend their time answering attacks in the religious and secular press, they would have little time left for the work of reconstruction. It is hard enough to keep pace with private correspondence. One of the most frustrating tasks of a bishop is answering letters from earnest extremists. Hours are consumed in explaining to Latinists that use of the vernacular does not really mean that the Church has sold out to the Protestants and, on the other hand, assuring vernacularists that although the canon of the Mass is not yet recited aloud in English this does not mean that the bishops have betrayed Pope John. Bishops although tempted to fall back on stereotyped replies are reluctant to act so impersonally.

It is suggested by their critics that bishops are remote men, untroubled by the struggles and aspirations of their priests and people. In fact the greater part of a bishop's day is spent meeting priests and people or dealing with their letters. Bishops should not be pictured as bureaucrats unfeelingly administering a diocese, when not presiding austerely at pontifical functions in cathedrals. If this were a true picture bishops would indeed be out of touch with reality. A man who leads only a public life must remain unaware of what people think and feel. Today, as it happens, a bishop, even if he never stirred from his desk, could hardly be unaware of what his people think. Almost every week letters from Catholics are in the correspondence columns of newspapers. Those who write regularly to the press are not ordinary people. Once or twice in a lifetime a private person may write to an editor—usually under stress of emotion. The inveterate correspondents, on the other hand, are men and women who feel that they have a mission. They believe it to be their duty to give their informed views to the world at large. These people are not necessarily self-opinionated, cranky or conceited. It is only that they are different from normal people who, like them, often feel the urge to write to the press but, unlike them, usually overcome it.

Hundreds of priests and people write privately to their bishop. They provide him with a fairly wide view of feeling within the Church. Most bishops also receive letters of complaint and opinions on every imaginable theological or social topic. Such correspondence, together with articles in journals and reviews, would acquaint a bishop with the likes and dislikes of his priests and people even if he never mixed with them. But, of course, he does. Most of my time as a bishop is spent in the pastoral visitation of churches, schools, hospitals and the homes of the sick and old.

During the first eighteen months following the Council, attacks on the bishops by articulate Catholics were fairly continuous. They accused the bishops of refusing to implement the decrees of the Council. They showed no awareness of the bishops' obligation to study closely the likely effects of proposed changes before issuing definitive instructions. It was not by chance that the Council left the time and manner of implementing conciliar decrees to local hierarchies. The Church has a store of wisdom after centuries of experience of Councils. The Second Vatican Council was not the first nor the most important Council in history.

The Church of Rome is often alleged to be monolithic. It is, in fact, no more monolithic than human nature. Knowledge is objective but good teachers adapt it to the age and intelligence of their pupils. Statesmen similarly know that objectively sound democratic legislation must be tempered to the state of development of emerging nations. Cruel consequences may follow the intemperate granting of independence though, of course, colonial powers have used this as an excuse for retaining control. Nevertheless it remains true that the evils of colonization are rarely cured by abrupt abdication. It may require heroism to resist local tyrants clamouring for power. Most hierarchies immediately after the Council had to withstand the clamour of a few for the sake of the whole people of God. Enthusiasm is excellent but it is no substitute for pastoral training and experience.

The Catholics of England can with complete respect be compared with the citizens of an emerging nation. They are still amazingly dependent upon the clergy. The etymology of the word 'cleric' or 'clerk' is enlightening. A clerk was a man able to read. Historically he was a priest or monk. In the English common law the Benefit of Clergy was the right of exemption from trial by a secular court. Subsequently it came to mean exemption from sentence when convicted on a first offence. Literate citizens were too few for the community to be able to afford to lock them up or kill them off. Since the clergy were almost the only educated people, what is now

called paternalism was forced upon them. After Tudor times
the clerical monopoly of education began to disappear. By
the eighteenth century literacy was general except among the
very poor. In the last century the Catholic population being
preponderantly poor was educationally backward. The
Catholic faith had died out among the common people of
England. It revived partly through conversions but mainly as
a result of the Irish famine.

A hundred years ago most Catholics were fugitives from
the Irish famine. There were always Catholic enclaves in
Lancashire, Yorkshire and Northumberland, but it was the
Irish who re-established the faith in English industrial towns.
Naturally they brought with them their social and religious
traditions. The priest had always been looked on as their
protector. He had stood by them in the darkest hours and
was deservedly regarded as a father. They looked to the priest
as a guide in all their affairs. In poor districts even in our own
day this dependence of Catholic people on their priests per-
sists. This fact has to be taken into consideration when we
study the impact of the Council on the Catholic community in
England. In countries where the faithful have been less dependent on clergy the lay responsibility envisaged by the
Council is grasped more easily than in countries like our own.
Priests in general are less reluctant to divest themselves of
power than is their flock to assume it.

Catholics living in a scholastic environment—I forbear to
call them intellectuals because that title, being now claimed
by almost everyone literate, has acquired a pejorative con-
notation—are only rarely aware of the delicate nature of
pastoral responsibility. They frequently confuse academic
freedom with unrestricted freedom of action. Knowing that
scholarship cannot flourish without research they easily come
to believe that intellectual restraint is in all circumstances
undesirable. Every man, they feel, always has the right to say

exactly what he thinks. This is not true. The more responsible a man's position the less free he is to speak without
careful thought—especially on subjects in which he has no
special competence. A curate can afford to define dogmatic
truth more often than a cardinal. Increase of knowledge and
responsibility is restricting. Those in authority are morally
bound to speak circumspectly. They need not play the
coward but they have to practise charity towards those who
depend upon them. An undergraduate may say what he likes
on any subject. He usually does. Nobody is likely to be guided
by his words. A wise professor, however freely he may
express himself in the senior common room, will weigh his
words when addressing his own students. A bishop must
often keep silent rather than risk causing confusion in the
minds of his flock.

After a bishops' meeting early in 1967, a Catholic paper
reported that the hierarchy had met to discuss plans for
implementing the Council 'behind closed doors'. It is a
revealing phrase. The inference is that bishops offend against
some elementary principle of justice by holding confidential
discussions. It is as if they were an ecclesiastical cabal plot-
ting against the freedom-loving flock. A Cabinet meeting does not attract notice in the press by being held behind
closed doors. All responsible leaders as a matter of course
have confidential discussions before making public announce-
ments. This complaint against private meetings of the bishops
betrays a lack of trust. Yet the Council's Constitution on
the Church says: 'For their part the faithful must cling to
their bishop as the Church does to Christ and Jesus Christ
to the Father, so that everything may harmonize in unity'
(Section 22).

Occasionally a section of the laity displays positive contempt for the shepherds of the flock. Episcopal pronouncements are seized upon by angry rather than hungry sheep.

Before the Council the Catholic Church in this country was the admiration of visitors from the continent. The love and trust between the faithful and clergy were the object of envy. French visitors especially were astonished to find a community in which anti-clericalism was unknown. They would exhort us to preserve, at all costs, our parochial schools which they took to be the basis of the remarkable harmony between priests and people.

The picture is less attractive today. But it is not so unpleasant as strangers might gather from the writing of those out of sympathy with the Catholic way of life in this island. For the first time this century, bishops are attacked by laymen in bitterly personal fashion. It is forgotten that the bishops did not offer themselves for election. Candidates seek political office because presumably they believe themselves to be specially fitted to become legislators. Thus the victor in an election may expect eventually to become the target for criticism. The unfortunate man chosen to be a bishop, on the other hand, is less a victor than a victim. Clergy are not likely to manœuvre for high office. A married clergy may legitimately look for advancement if only for the sake of the family and especially for their children's education. A Catholic priest would have no such worthy motive. When as an act of obedience to the pope he consents to become a bishop he is not thirsting for power. A mitre will most likely prove to be a crown of thorns.

Devout laymen are alarmed by the unprecedented bitterness of recent attacks on their Fathers in God. In certain circles it has become socially dangerous to speak charitably of bishops. Before the Council Catholics had a touching reverence for their priest and considered it bad form to refer to him by his unadorned surname. Today a bishop is fortunate if he is referred to by nothing worse. It is droll that those who attack the bishops most vehemently claim to speak with the spirit of Pope John. Good Pope John unaffectedly loved his brother bishops. That is one reason why he summoned them to Rome. He was hopeful that the Council would last only one session. He thought of it as the diocesan Synod of Rome on a larger scale. He loved to gather his venerable brethren around him. He used to ask us if we thought it would be necessary to have a second session. He grieved at being responsible for keeping bishops away from their priests and people. With prophetic insight he foresaw the danger of divisions. Mercifully, God called him before he saw his brethren in the episcopate become the object of attack by their own sons.

Opponents of the hierarchy are sometimes sincere Catholics whose outlook has been distorted by the intemperate writing of the early period of the Council. This gave a wrong direction to their thinking. They naively accepted the journalists' story that most bishops resented the Council and were determined to annul its decrees. Even to this day they do not appreciate that the almost unanimous votes in favour of the decrees disprove the alleged opposition of the Fathers. They were assured by mainly clerical commentators that at the conclusion of the Council the bishops would return to their sees with a common if unspoken agreement to stifle all new ideas and restore 'normal' conditions. Reforms would have to be wrung from them.

Some of the laity therefore resolved to become watchdogs for the Church of the aggiornamento. Every delay in producing plans for the post-conciliar Church was interpreted as a deliberate attempt by the bishops to block the road to renewal. These men and women are undoubtedly on fire with zeal. Their original mistake has been to accept a caricature of the episcopate. They have not grasped that the Council was, in fact, the Fathers of the Council whose minds were subjected to the action of the Holy Spirit. It is true that at first some bishops, bewildered by the temper of the debates, felt that the Council was inopportune. Before the Council ended, however, the bishops almost without exception were enthusiastic for what the Council had accomplished. The voice of the Council was for them the voice of God. As faithful sons of the Church they pledged themselves to carry out whatever the Church had commanded. Delays in putting decrees into practice are the result not of ill-will but of prudence. The Church would be ill served if bishops were to give way to impatient critics and promulgate regulations which would not stand the test of time.

It would be disingenuous to suggest that the present turmoil in the Church is all the fault of a few laymen and religious anxious to usurp the place of the bishops as guides of the faithful. There is no simple explanation of the present distress. It would be unchristian to cast stones at each other in smug self-righteousness. None of us is without sin or blame. The chief fault of those in authority is a failure to admit that before the Council power in the Church was sometimes autocratic. Superiors were usually kindly enough men and women but the traditional manner of exercising authority was itself often harsh. It is notorious that ecclesiastical administration treated priests and people if not as pawns at least as conscripts. Their duty was to obey orders without question. Bishops sometimes told priests what they must do, without thinking it necessary to explain the reasons behind the instructions. Parish priests, in turn, were accustomed to command curates and parishioners without concession to the democratic spirit of our times.

We now realize that this chain of authority stretching from Rome to the smallest parish was too rigid and impersonal. Before the Council, obedience was the chief consideration in the minds of both rulers and ruled. The clergy, in particular, were men under authority and the bishop was not unlike the centurion in the gospel. The bishops themselves were also subject to authority. Before the Council they were allowed little discretion in much of their pastoral work. Every five years the Holy See issued a list of faculties which really did no more than give them the privilege of discharging their duties. It now seems strange that few bishops resented the frequent need to seek permission from Rome for trivial acts of jurisdiction. In the pre-conciliar Church the behaviour of bishops was patterned on that of higher authority. That is the explanation of their apparent lack of trust in the good sense of their priests and people.

The Church rarely moves with the times. That, in fact, is the explanation of the so-called paternalism of the Church. It largely reflects the social habits of an earlier generation. We must not forget that until recently most children were brought up in an atmosphere of near hostility. In school they were beaten for being stupid. When not being watched by teachers they were controlled by prefects whose main duty was to detect and punish misdemeanours. In a few schools these customs in some measure still prevail. Towards the adolescents of the last generation mistrust increased. Left to themselves, parents assumed, their sons and daughters would almost certainly misbehave. After the war liberalizing principles were introduced into homes, schools and even borstals and prisons. In most of these communities the beating stopped. Psychology asserted its influence and those in authority were astonished to discover that trust usually produces better results than threats of punishment. Loosening of discipline inevitably has had some unfortunate results. Society has not yet found a mean between harshness and indulgence. Perhaps we are still reacting against Victorian severity and prudery.

Until the Council taught us the need to be more loving the

old attitudes survived. Those in authority had not lacked compassion. They were not tyrants so much as slaves to a system. It is not surprising if some superiors feel uncertain of themselves now that the old system is breaking up. It would be unreasonable to expect those who have spent a lifetime in the old ways to be able to readjust themselves in a matter of months. It may be salutary for those in revolt against what they regard as the unduly slow pace of reform to consider what some of our nuns had to endure before the Council decreed the renewal of religious life. Of all Catholics our Sisters are the most esteemed by the public at large. Few outsiders, however, realize the restrictions under which they sometimes live. These splendid women give up their freedom to serve the rest of God's people. In schools, hospitals, orphanages and the homes of the poor they serve Christ uncomplainingly. Before the Council their holy Rule often made almost inhuman demands. Their personal liberty was so restricted as virtually not to exist. By leaving their families and friends they had bartered human for divine love and few concessions were made to their natural desire to visit parents and relatives. By their own choice cloistered nuns still maintain this complete detachment but most Congregations have in some measure restored daughters to their families.

The constitutions of all religious orders are being revised. Thought is being given to the personal freedom and dignity of the members. It was once considered destructive of religious life to allow nuns to take a cup of tea with the laity. Some were forbidden to take refreshments even with Sisters belonging to another community. Nuns were regimented in almost every detail of their daily lives. Few can have suspected that these smiling nuns were practising constant mortification through the Rule of life they had embraced. Yet they were rarely sorry for themselves. Even after the aggiornamento most nuns are far more concerned to preserve a rule of life than to seek relaxations. Their overriding desire is to keep themselves unspotted from this world in order to be close to Christ their Spouse and serve him in their brethren. Bitterness is rare among nuns, but they suffered more than any from the pre-conciliar outlook in the Church.

In this there is a lesson for us all. One great weakness revealed by the Council was the absence of love in the exercise of authority. Superiors often lacked imagination and for this reason seemed to act unfeelingly. Present-day critics do not appreciate that those following a faulty system need not personally have been at fault. Christlike obedience was the ideal. Neither those who gave orders nor those who received them thought of questioning the wisdom of the Rule. That, of course, does not excuse the inhumanity of those superiors who refused to discuss grievances. Impersonal commands, prohibitions and excommunications are now admitted to be unworthy of superiors in a Church claiming to be the Body of Christ who ruled by love. Contempt and bitterness in those under authority are equally inexcusable. Obedience is as necessary in the post-conciliar Church as it has been throughout her history. Without humility there can be no approach to Christ. Because he was humble Christ was obedient. Those who belittle the virtue of obedience deny Christ. Followers of Christ owe loving obedience to all who stand in his place. He was made obedient even to the death of the cross. A true Christian may follow no other path.

Three

Rosemary Haughton

Dear Father John,

You suggested that this second part of our book should be like two 'letters', in which we would talk directly to each other, commenting on each other's essays, and taking the discussion a stage further. I think this is a good idea. For one thing, the very fact of doing so makes it clear that we think of each other as people. So much Catholic writing, even when people are meant to be 'discussing', is not addressed *to* people but across them. They have to be there, because somebody has to buy the book—but that's all. This isn't that kind of book. It is a dialogue, words between two. Only two, of course. You are one bishop. You are the most important one in England but you are only one. You don't (thank God) tell the other bishops what to do. Some of them may not even agree with your initiative in writing this book. This is one bishop talking to one lay person, and I am possibly less representative of 'the laity' than you are of 'the clergy'. Never mind—the important thing is that we really are doing it, and if we can do it so can others. We are not ambassadors, or representatives, or symbols, we are just people. But we are also Christians, and that is why we want to talk. We want to help a little to restore the bond of charity in the Church, because unless the Church is living by the love of Christ she cannot preach the love of Christ. The preaching of the gospel has always been done by the language of living as much as by the spoken or written word, and if the Church's words are not to be manifest nonsense they must say what her life means.

In a way, this is what both our papers are about—unity and love, love shown in unity, unity through love, and the articulation of these, which is authority.

Your own paper gives two excellent examples of unity. You were right to remind us of the time before the Council, of the severe discipline that clergy and laity accepted, usually with patience and love, for the sake of unity. The discipline of our Church was the envy of other Churches, you said. It was enviable, because (with sad exceptions) it was truly an expression of love. There were exaggerations, there was persecution of the non-conformist, there was timidity and suspicion and therefore little theological growth. The nuns whom you write about suffered restrictions that, looking back, seem almost unbelievable, and a great waste. Yet they, and all the others, not only accepted them but very many grew by them in holiness, and that means in love. So much that was obviously inhuman and harsh and unnecessary— and out of it so much love! But it isn't strange, because the suppressed theologians and the hungry curates and the restricted nuns and the over-dominated laity saw the things that made them suffer as *necessary*. All these seemed inevitable to them, and therefore they had to be suffered for the sake of the Christ's kingdom. So these things could indeed produce unity—the true unity which happens when people are doing something they feel is worth doing and can therefore ignore incidental suffering. 'A woman in labour suffers because her time is come, but afterwards she forgets her pain, she is so happy that her child is born.' Christ knew very well that no suffering is unbearable if it seems necessary in order to achieve something worthwhile.

We have no need to forget, or be ashamed of, the pre-conciliar Church. It was marred by power-politics, intrigue and callousness, as it always has been and always will be, but it displayed a unity which was often (though not always) a unity of love, not of fear. The discipline, the humility, the obedience—they were all the result of the conviction that personal disappointment and pain were unimportant compared with the unity of the Church as a living sign of God's will for mankind.

The other example you give of real unity in love is your account of the Council, a very illuminating one for people who only read about it in the press. This is a first-hand impression, you were really there. And even more striking in this account than what you say about the various documents is the impression you give of having shared a tremendous experience. Clearly, it changed your life, your outlook, your understanding of your vocation. It seems to have done this for most of the bishops. And it is easy to see why. You were all working *together*, at something that seemed increasingly worthwhile, increasingly exciting. There must have been long stretches of boredom, many moments of exasperation and frustration, times of gloom and foreboding, or at least of intense anxiety. Above all, there must have been constant fatigue, and the harassing knowledge of work piling up at home (and an unfortunate inability to bi-locate efficiently!). But you say nothing about all this—clearly, it didn't matter, it was unimportant compared with what was being done, a work that drew everyone together into a deep and enduring unity that will last through long—perhaps permanent—separation. In such an atmosphere it was possible for people to admit ignorance, and to learn, without any feeling of humiliation. Everyone was learning, everyone was equal, above all everyone was called by God to a great and urgent task which—however huge—could be undertaken because it was clearly his will. This was real unity, and real love.

Perhaps the most interesting sentence in this part of your essay is the one that says: 'In four years there were not half a dozen serious clashes and *these did no harm to fraternal charity.*' Yet there were deep and serious disagreements, and some of them must have caused the bishops who disagreed considerable agony of mind. The atmosphere of brotherly love was not due to docility—you show this clearly when you describe the rejection of the first schema on the missions. These were men who felt strongly, even passionately, and were prepared to say so without mincing their words. Some of the speeches that reached us through the press made most exhilarating reading, they were so clearly from the heart. And when people feel deeply and violently they disagree—openly, as you describe. But, with exceptions, these fiercely worded disagreements did *not* lead to bitterness or division. On the contrary, 'the unity among Catholic bishops . . . is little short of miraculous'.

Why was there this unity, this real brotherly love among men of diverse origins, attainments and ideas, men accustomed to rule, to make decisions? Surely there was unity because you *trusted* each other. You were, indeed, brothers, sharing the same calling, the same burden, the same task, in all its many forms. On a basis of respect and trust and shared enthusiasm you could oppose each other, argue, plead, even shout at each other—and all this would lead not to estrangement but to greater understanding and dedication.

The two examples (equally real) of unity that I chose from your essay show very different ways of achieving it. Would *you*, a bishop, have been content if the first kind—unity expressed as docility and passive obedience—had been im-

posed on you and your brother bishops at the Council?
Would the Council have been so fruitful if your ideas had
been ignored, if the only way you had been allowed to show
loyalty and love had been by quiet agreement with the pre-
prepared schemata? That *could* have been a real gesture of
love—and, as you point out, bishops before the Council were
used to working under just this kind of authority. But was
that the kind of expression of unity that seemed right, to you
and the other bishops at the Council? Clearly, this did not
seem to you an adequate expression of the role of bishops in
the Church, nowadays. Nor did you feel you were being disloyal to the Pope by rejecting such a form of authority. And,
clearly, you were justified. *That* expression of unity, *that*
language of authority, was not the right one for the times, and
you knew it.

The bishop and his people
Now I'm going to be unjust. I know, because I've met you
and talked to you, that you don't really feel like this—but
the *impression* that is given to ordinary Catholics, both
clerical and lay, is that most of the bishops are not prepared
to accept the same sort of expression of unity among the
people of God in their own countries as they experienced
among themselves during the Council. Among themselves
they discovered a *new* kind of unity, and therefore a con-
vincing and meaningful way realizing *authority*. But when it
comes to relations with other Catholics they seem to expect
people to express unity in the old way. They want them to
go on understanding authority (their relation to their author,
Christ) in a way which the bishops themselves have discovered by experience to be inadequate to meet the occasion.
And when Catholics don't want to do so—when *they* want
to disagree and discuss and protest and shout—then the
bishops get worried and talk about a crisis of authority. I

know there is a big difference. The bishops were all people
with the same job, the same degree of responsibility, the same
power. But a bishop among his people is there to rule, however he interprets that word. So they aren't a group of
brothers in quite the same sense. He has to make the final
decision—or if he doesn't it is he who empowers someone
else to do so. Yet to say they are *not* brothers would be mon-
strous. Before a man is a bishop he is a Christian, he and
his people are brothers in Christ, 'fellow workers with God',
'co-heirs with Christ', 'a nation of priests'. They *should* be
able to express unity in the same way as the bishops did at
the Council, and not only as Catholics did *before* the Council.

I think a lot of people—not just bishops by any means—
are afraid that to be on such terms of equality would be to
endanger the sense of authority in the Church and lose that
discipline which, as you say, other Christians used to admire.

Let me give you a very homely example from my own experience. I have worked with my husband in the theatre of the
school where he teaches. When a big production is being prepared the boys taking part—stage-hands, electricians, car-
penters and so on, as well as actors and musicians—have to
be given extra time off from other things; they get into old
clothes, between times they brew tea, they have a freedom
that other boys lack. Sometimes they work quite late at night.
The atmosphere is very relaxed, boys and masters talk as
equals, tease each other, and work together. There are few
obvious signs of outward respect for the masters, and everyone (including me) gets so dirty that it might sometimes be
hard for an outsider to tell which they are, anyway. Because
of all this some people feel (or used to feel) that working in
the theatre undermines the boys' respect for authority, and
their sense of discipline. But the fact is that it would be hard
to find a set-up with a greater sense of discipline. When a job
needs to be finished in a hurry, everyone helps, no matter

how much free time is given up or how tired they get. Never mind what their 'proper' job or their status is—they all work, and under authority *obey*, at once, because this is how the work is best done, and they care about it. But each carries responsibility for the rest—if he does his job badly everyone will lose by it, and he knows this, and responds—sometimes by efforts of which no one (even himself) had thought him capable. Sometimes tempers are lost. Sometimes high spirits get out of hand, sometimes the sheer exhilaration of achievement overflows into silliness. But no lasting harm is done, no bitterness is left, because the sense of sharing in a common work which everyone cares about is stronger than any personal failure or fault. And the sense of unity that happens through all this—the experience of real community—is something that for many is unique in their school lives. The experience, in fact, has the same kind of quality, in its own way, as you found in the experience of the Council in a much greater way. Yet this community inside a school consists of a mixture of people *in* authority and *under* authority. And this authority is not impaired but greatly strengthened, because the bond is woven of shared difficulties and shared jokes and of personal affection and respect and the warmth of a common goal and a common achievement. In this atmosphere people can accept criticism, admit failure, make and receive suggestions, protest, complain, swear, argue—or shut up, and all this without lasting resentment or humiliation.

This is only one tiny example. But I think it is a valid one and can be applied to a bigger community. You mention especially the 'turmoil' in Holland which has caught the attention of the press. You pay tribute to the courage and also to the fervour of the Dutch, and yet you seem to feel that people may be scandalized at the news from Holland. Perhaps there are many who 'deplore' the Dutch situation, but it seems that Cardinal Alfrink at least is not worried, if he suggests that 'the Dutch merely speak openly of matters which Catholics elsewhere discuss in secret'. Precisely. This is what you did at the Council—with such astounding results. Perhaps what is happening in Holland is not *in spite* of the fervour of the Dutch but *because* of it. As you say, the unrest is not merely in the Church. The Dutch royal family, in fact the whole society, are feeling it. They are all experiencing the search for a new language of authority. But the outcome need not be anarchy. It may be a new and more Christian understanding of what makes a community.

Again, to comfort us for what we may feel is our own slow progress, you give a depressing description of the situation in Germany. Actually, I think there may be fewer people than you suppose who have this naïve idea that continental Catholics are galloping ahead while England stagnates. (Anyone who reads *New Blackfriars* or *Slant* must have a very different impression.) However that may be, the description you give of the German scene is of a community (if one can call it that) that has *not* learned to share, so that when they do come together all they can do is mouth at each other from behind barriers of mutual incomprehension. In any case, it is clear that the German bishops are having great difficulty in creating among their own people the sense of enthusiasm they discovered among themselves at the Council.

On the other hand, as you point out, there is theological unrest in Austria and Germany, and the bishops have warned against its excesses. And you point out that when unorthodox theology is slung about, the bishops have to protest and warn.

Here we come to the heart of the matter, which affects us in England too.

At this point I am going to be frank almost to danger point, because I can't see any other way of making clear what I think is the real 'trouble' in this country.

You said at the beginning of your paper that nobody can

be completely objective, and because you know this I know you realize the immense influence of the unspoken assumptions that underlie one's opinions and words. So now I want to point out what seem to me to be certain unspoken assumptions that underlie your essay, and also the attitudes of many other people in authority in the Church, here and abroad. They are more destructive of unity, greater blocks to progress, than any deliberate authoritarianism. They are all the more so because they underlie real and generous and enthusiastic efforts at co-operation and progress in the Church. Many bishops, indeed, are much more 'progressive' and infinitely more dedicated to renewal than some of the laity or 'lower' clergy. They can't make out why they seem to meet a blank wall of distrust or a barrage of abuse, when they seem to themselves to be going flat out to get things done.

There are a few key phrases in your essay which are symptoms of what I mean: 'the exuberant irresponsibility of some Catholic writing since the Council', 'false thinking on the Eucharist'; and others like this. And the clear assumption that unrest comes from the young, is natural to them, and will be outgrown.

Perhaps you remember that when we first met, and planned this book, you told me that you did not mind how 'outrageous' I was in my expressed opinions. I know what you meant—you wanted it to be clear in the book that I was saying what I really thought, and was not concealing my true opinions out of deference to your authority. You wanted people to realize that we really could *talk*. I took this as it was meant, an expression of genuine trust and friendship and openness, and was grateful. But underlying this remark was the assumption that if I (or people like me) expressed ideas about the Church and the faith that were violently or 'shockingly' different from the way you, and many others, express these things, then such an expression must be *off-centre* in some way, at least possibly 'unorthodox'. The assumption is that the way of thinking that has been *usual* is therefore central, orthodox and responsible, while *unusual* expressions are likely to be, though perhaps quite harmless, anyway less surely orthodox. Now the new opinions may well be unorthodox, but *so may the older ones*. We now realize that some long-accepted interpretations of Catholic doctrine are far from orthodox. (For instance, the notion that all pagans, etc. go to hell.) On the other hand that huge pillar of orthodoxy, St Thomas Aquinas, was, in his time, considered to be an outrageous innovator, a menace to sound doctrine, a heretic, etc. etc. Possibly, those who were prepared to tolerate but not approve him described his efforts as the result of 'exuberant irresponsibility'! Such a description assumes that theological speculation of a violently new kind is more likely than not to be irresponsible. I am not saying that it cannot be. Perhaps it often is, but the clinging to traditional modes can be just as irresponsible because it can protect people from real thinking, when they most need this challenge. Cowardice is just as irresponsible as 'brashness'. It is not newness or oldness that makes theology responsible or irresponsible, orthodox or unorthodox, but the degree of its careful and prayerful orientation towards Christ's teaching, revealed to us through the Church's developing life.

New ideas are disturbing, even shocking. They may hurt people who are accustomed to older versions. This is inevitable and therefore those who propose them should try to minimize the hurt. But the degree of shock caused by an idea is not a sufficient index of its degree of orthodoxy or unorthodoxy. It is arguable that when an idea is new the onus of demonstrating its orthodoxy lies on its proposer, but in that case there must be a climate of thought in which he is able to do so. And he cannot do so if he is *assumed* to be, at least probably, irresponsible, just because what he is saying is new or disturbing or even shocking.

Again, some of the new teaching on the Eucharist may indeed be utterly false (and therefore quite ephemeral). But so often a way of expressing the tradition that seems at first likely to mislead the faithful may contain an idea which is true and needs to be developed. Then it will cease to mislead. This was especially true for instance of the modernist doctrines. They were mainly and clearly unorthodox but there was in them a seed of truth which has since grown and flowered. (Even in heresy there is this seed of truth, which is precisely what makes it attractive.) At the moment some theologians are experimenting with a new use of words, a whole new philosophical system, as a tool for conveying the gospel message. It is as shockingly new to us as St Thomas's use of Aristotle was shockingly new to his Platonist contemporaries. In exploring their system, these theologians are bound to follow some paths that prove to be dead ends. But if they are to discover the way ahead they must be encouraged to go on exploring *all* paths, and so find out which is the true one. If their adventures into untrodden ways are immediately labelled 'youthful curiosity', 'irresponsible', 'immature' if not downright 'unorthodox', they naturally begin to feel that it is hopeless to try to get those in authority to understand what they are at. They relapse into cynicism, or have nervous breakdowns, or continue in a bubble of carefully preserved personal euphoria which they dare not break.

I am not saying that none of the new ways are irresponsible or unorthodox. Maybe some are, maybe even (though I don't think so), they *all* are. But even if it were so the cure for irresponsibility is to be given responsibility, as every schoolmaster knows. The cure for immaturity is to be given a mature role.

But there is another interesting thing about this 'theological unrest'. Theological speculation is not now, as it has often been in the past, the pursuit of a smallish world of scholars, while the rest of Catholic life flows on unheeding. On the contrary, the impulse that has driven Catholic writers, including quite unofficial ones, to explore new ways of expressing Catholic truth has been their vivid sense of the vocation of the *whole* Church, as the people of God. The experiments in eucharistic theology have grown straight out of the need to renew the Church's sense of the Eucharist as the heart of her life—and not just the heart in the static sense of the centre and symbol, but the heart as the source of its life, literally forcing ever-renewed life-blood through the huge and complex network of its body. There have been times when the body of the Church displayed all the symptoms of a 'blue baby' whose damaged heart cannot pump with sufficient force to give full, energetic life.

The same need to rediscover community—not as an end in itself but as a means to preaching the gospel now—has led to experiments in parochial structure, to various forms of 'worker priest' movements, to the 'secular institutes'. It has also led to the controversial effort to express human community as Christian, in Marxist terms. Those who do this are trying to show the Church's role clearly as a sign for the modern world. It should be that sign by being in the world and of it, and showing that hopes and plans that might otherwise seem un-Christian, or even anti-Christian, can be the means of preaching Christ's gospel to a torn and selfish world. All these things are dangerous, they could, and do, allow people to lose sight of Christ. But also they can bring him into places and among people who never dreamt that he could be anything but the self-justification of those whom privilege has made indifferent to suffering.

The 'way out' theological speculation in Germany and Austria seems to be an attempt to break through the very isolation and indifference which the bishops in those countries find so frustrating. It may be 'brash', but it is alive, it shows the Church is alive. In Holland, where it has been given its head to an almost unprecedented extent, the result has been (with some very undesirable squabbling) also an almost unprecedented interest and enthusiasm among ordinary Catholics. And, as you say, the altar rails are crowded.

Of *course* the bishops have to warn against false doctrine, that is part of their work and I don't suppose they enjoy it much. But if, besides warning, they could also pick out the underlying motives and encourage them and give them scope, their comments would be more helpful—not only to the writers and theologians, but to the many puzzled and worried Catholics who wonder what the blazes the Church is coming to these days.

This brings me back to the 'simple faithful'. They are harried and bewildered, hurt by what seems the lack of faith of 'intellectuals', made miserable by attacks on the value of what they have always loved, or else bitterly and defiantly determined to oppose all that is new.

There was an elderly woman who wrote to me: her faith had been chilled and her peace of mind rocked by a feeling that all that she had grown up with and loved—rosary, statues, Lourdes water, medals and so on—were 'stupid, ridiculous superstitions', as she said, and that the 'progressives' were destroying the Church she knew. 'I felt really terrified I would lose my faith,' she said. 'I couldn't understand why some of the progressives seemed to *want* to be hurtful and to confuse.' But later she added: 'Since *then* I have tried to understand, and now feel that the strong wind of change blowing through the Church can only do good.' She showed, in the same letter, that she was realizing the reason why some of the things she loved, and which brought

her to God, could be, for others, obstacles and even scandals.
She was prepared to accept this difference, and look beyond
it to a common faith and hope. This change—from fear and
hurt to confidence and understanding and hope—happened
because someone explained what was going on, and why,
with affection and respect. The point is that what people
(even the 'simplest') need is not protection but *trust*. This
letter is not unusual. One man who described himself as 'a
not very bright ordinary working man', was eventually able
to say that he now 'understood what it's all about'. Anyone
can help who comes across people who are worried or
puzzled. Even by letter—a poor second best—much can be
done. A time of upheaval and change is painful for many, but
these many are Christians, they are the people of God, living
by his Spirit. When we speak to each other we are speaking
to each other in that Spirit. So barriers of fear are broken
down, personal tastes seem trivial, personal suffering matters
less, we begin to share a vision and a hope, we can go forward together, respecting and protecting each other's sensitive spots, aware of many things on which we cannot agree
and never could, but loving each other all the same.

This kind of experience is important. When you start to
meet people on this level it is astonishing how differences
don't matter. It isn't that one ignores them, or thinks them
unimportant, but they are not really an obstacle to the knowledge of a shared life and a shared hope. In a way, they make
the unity stronger, because the effort needed to overcome
one's prejudices (or impatience or fears) makes the bond that
is discovered more a matter of real love and less a question
of simply feeling at ease with people one happens to agree
with.

But this only happens if we treat each other as equals, as
brothers in Christ. Our Lord addressed his twelve as 'little
children', to show his love and care for them, but he didn't

treat them as children. He sent them out on their first preaching mission—alone—to deliver his message. He staked his *own* reputation and the success of his mission on this handful of enthusiastic but only briefly trained young men. That was how they learned. Yet so often, now, the most sincerely devoted clergy think of the needed change in their attitude to other Catholics as a change from being *severe* parents to being kind and understanding parents. But they aren't parents in *that* sense at all, and their people are not children, in any sense. Priests are 'parents' in that they can give life. This is not their gift alone, but all God's people share it. They are the signs of this power of life-giving, as I suggested when I was talking about what authority is. This life they support, encourage, revive. In this sense they are truly 'fathers'. But the relationship is one of spiritual, not psychological, fatherhood. I suppose it is the feeling that their people are their children in the psychological sense of being necessarily dependant and immature that makes it natural to assume that unrest and questioning are essentially a symptom of youth, and can therefore be treated with understanding and indulgence but not taken seriously. In fact, some of the most 'turbulent' priests and laymen at the moment are middle-aged. They may be right or wrong, but to put down the cause of their turbulence to youth, or even persistent immaturity, is to beg the question. The question is not, are they young (or immature or hot-headed or exuberant or whatever) but are they *right*?

I am not excusing lack of charity from lay people, or silliness, or the sort of 'brutal and triumphalist radicalism' which Herbert McCabe castigated in his famous editorial. He was right to notice and condemn the 'new élite of right-thinking people', which really does 'stifle critical judgement'. This sort of thing is very nasty, by any standards. And it can and does provoke exactly the wrong (though extremely understandable) reaction from the bishops and clergy—I mean the kind of reaction that might be described as paternal self-control.

When the Corinthians got to bickering and lobbying and splitting into parties (each claiming to be 'right-thinking', of course), St Paul wrote them a letter that must have made them writhe. It wasn't restrained and dignified, it was just angry, agonized and palpably hurt. Obviously, it did the trick. It got through to them. They knew he cared, enough to forget his dignity.

I once heard a parish priest tell his congregation they were a lot of lazy, smug, etc. etc. The effect was electric. They loved him, they knew he cared, not from 'above', but right in among them, in their flesh and bones, so that he personally minded their weakness and apathy. Harmony is good, courtesy is good, but one can pay too high a price for it, when the price is loss of real charity. There is no virtue in invective, but there is much virtue in the bond of brotherly love that dares to let fly, because people care for each other so much that they dare not be silent. And this applies both to those in authority and those under authority. Peter was the chief of the apostles, but when Paul thought Peter was wrong he went to him and said so, openly. Nobody supposed that this detracted from Peter's real authority—rather, it was a correction of his failure to exercise a true authority. He had the humility to accept the rebuke. Yet now we seem to feel that even when the Curia manifestly abuses its authority, to say so is somehow disloyal. Even if the Curia's authority were actually that of the pope himself, must we never, now, 'withstand Peter to his face'? Can a pope never make a mistake or commit a sin? The maintenance of a pious fiction to this effect is surely very unhealthy.

I suppose what I am suggesting is that we really want something much nearer to the atmosphere of the early Church than to that of nineteenth century Catholicism. Not because it is necessarily intrinsically better but because it fits the needs of the time. Only a failure to read the New Testament could make one suppose that the first decades of the Church were a period of unblemished fervour and peace. There were constant difficulties, rows, mistakes, feuds. To us, looking back, it seems obvious that the Church was going to come through it all. I don't suppose it seemed so obvious at the time.

Where we stand

Nowadays we wonder what will become of the Church. Will it dwindle to a persecuted minority, or change into a more loosely connected group of communities? We don't know. We don't *need* to know, any more than the early Church needed to foresee her future. In fact, the early Church's expectation of an imminent end to history is in one sense a very healthy state of mind, it helps to keep things in proportion. After all, whenever the end comes, the fact remains that 'the day of salvation is *now*'.

This is where we are. All this analysing of difficulties, these attempts to build bridges of understanding, to come together in love, to realize our brotherhood—these are not ends in themselves. They are 'for the sake of the kingdom of heaven'. So, finally, we must ask, what does this mean? What is the Church—here and now—for? Where are we going?

We are all given to speculating about the future, planning ahead. To some extent, we have to, but often pride grows from it, a conviction that *my* plans must be best. This is a disease that afflicts all sections of the Church and is at the root of most of the really intractable disagreements. Daniel Berrigan wrote:

'Many who call most energetically for change in the Church are among the least informed about the reality of the Church. They really expect the Church to "work" in

the way any large corporation is expected to work—or go
out of business. But, as a matter of fact, there is no promise
given by God that things will go well for us. Nor are our
criteria necessarily his. Neither history nor the bible
assures us that the Church will have the vitality or
imagination or moral passion to affect human life for the
better, in a large, perceptible sense. Utopia is not her
name. From the point of view of the person anxious for
change, refusing to face such hard talk may well mean a
refusal of the only promise God has really given us: "In
the world you will have suffering."

'And what follows? "I have overcome the world." Not
by a show of force, even of the icy moral rectitude of the
good Pharisee, but by a submission so radiantly pure that
it wins all conscience and assumes all hope to itself. There
is no other way, as Christian way.'[1]

When I read these words I realized that they were an echo
of the concluding words of your essay, rather as phrases of
the psalms often balance each other by saying the same thing
again, but in a different way so that each part illuminates the
other. I think this coincidence of thought is not a coincidence
in the sense of a chance and meaningless concurrence. Any
real thinking about the Church is bound to come to this:
obedience is the bond that makes us one in Christ. Not knowledge, or planning, or good organization—although they matter a lot, but just obedience. If that sounds a startling conclusion to a lot of talk about the need for freedom and trust
and responsibility and brotherhood, then I must again bring
in Father Berrigan, a man who has reason to know the meaning of obedience. (You wondered whether priests nowadays
who provoked sanctions would prove as humble as Teilhard
de Chardin. This one did. Also another, an Englishman.)

1. In *Truth and Consequence*, Sheed and Ward, London, 1967.

'The breathing area of freedom, and the discipline of obedience: both of them radically necessary in an age such as ours. The best men are proudly and passionately conscious of their dignity, and speak a great deal of their need of freedom; but in so speaking they express without saying it their longing for obedience, for someone to give themselves to, for communion and friendship, for a counterpoise of thought that will contain, interpret, and direct their experience.'

But we are Christians, our understanding of this counterpoise must not remain implicit only. We must say, clearly and with conviction, that obedience is the bond of love. Yes, but, 'authority is an organ of the authority of Christ when it, too, and more deeply and perhaps at greater cost to the one who obeys, is obedient to the Spirit'. I sometimes think that people in authority in the Church feel that those under authority get restless because their leaders ask too much of them. In that case, the leaders may feel that the best thing is to ask less. But the leader who is obedient to the Spirit may well have to ask not less but a great deal more. And this more will be given when the authority really is, clearly, the authority of Christ, expressing *his* mind.

'Tradition is brought to bear on the present when the imagination of Christ lives on, both in men of authority and in obedient men. What does it mean to live in the real world? The question is one that the Gospel both answers and refuses to answer: *answers* in the world experience of Christ, in his obedience and release into time. *Refuses* in its open ending: "Live on in me, as I in you." '

If the day of salvation is now, it means, also, here. It means this country, in the late sixties. It is here and now that we have to 'live on' in Christ, and recognize his life in us. I could go on quoting Daniel Berrigan, or any number of other great men. But they aren't writing this book. I am, and you are. What will it achieve? You don't know. I don't know. But I do know, and have learned much more deeply in writing it, that we are at a turning point of the history of the Church, when anything can happen. It's almost as if we were beginning again from the beginning. This is always true, in one sense, but now every circumstance is forcing us to see this.

At this time, then, we need to be vulnerable. We need to be able to feel the pushing of the Spirit and not to protect ourselves from him. But to do this we need each other. We aren't meant to carry out Christ's work alone. There are many gifts, and that means many opinions, abilities, temperaments. But one Spirit. We need all the diversity and we need to be aware of it, so that within it we can discern the real unity, for the greatest gift of the Spirit is love.

What does all this mean, in practice? It means we must be able to say what we think, but we must also listen, which is more difficult. (We must not be afraid that people 'outside' the Church will be shocked by disagreements. They are much more shocked by hypocritical agreement.) We must be able to rebuke (anybody) but also to accept rebuke (from anybody) without sulks. And that means both ways, *from* and *to* authority.

Then we must start taking the gospel literally. We must stop assuming that Christ's commands only 'really' apply to a selected few. This is false humility, and cowardice. We have to ask, honestly, '*Does* it mean *me*?' But in order to have the courage to answer such a question honestly, people need the support of their brethren. Now, especially, Christians may have to adopt unpopular positions or do unusually and even dramatically sacrificial things. If they take the gospel seriously they will do so. In that case the real unity of love is essential. People can't do this sort of thing alone—they would be very arrogant if they tried. They can do it because they are not just individuals but the Church. It is in this body that they have real power, which is not their own.

The common dedication

That is why trust matters so much, and why no differences must be allowed to mar it. When we, you and I, planned this book, and talked about it and other things, it must have been obvious to both of us that there were a lot of subjects about which we would never agree even if we talked for weeks, with the utmost candour and respect. There are those built-in attitudes in anyone's mind which shape all his thinking, however honest he is, and are only gradually modified. So I am sure there are ideas of mine which seem to you basically wrong, and there are ideas of yours which I feel I shall never understand. Yet we listened to each other, and I think both of us learned a lot. In the writing, and reading, of this book we have learned a lot more, our own ideas have grown. They have also, perhaps, grown closer together. (I feel they have, anyway.)

But more important than ideas is the sense of a common dedication. This belongs to the whole Church. We need it as never before, and when we need it we *have* it. God gives us what we need, when we need it. If only we will take hold of it. It isn't easy. It means both ruthless honesty and unlimited love. It means refusing to cover up scandals and corruption, but it also means not refusing to be identified with a Church that is often venal and despicable. It means avoiding double-think, yet not being self-righteous about the set-up that makes Vatican backstairs politics something we have learned to expect. It is unworthy of Christ's Church, and we should fight it—but this is *our* Church, this we are involved in totally, or else we have no right to speak because we have no power to love. What is wrong with the Church is not wrong with a group of people over there—so that we can thank God we are not as those intriguers and political machinators and fear-constrained oppressors. What is wrong is lack of love, and it happens because people are afraid—afraid of the removal of ancient supports. The only cure for this is love, and we can't give that from inside an enclave of enlightened self-righteousness. This is a worse darkness than that of the gothic gloom from which many fear to emerge. It isn't even humanly friendly. The sins of the Church are our sins, and they are all one sin—a refusal to love, whether from timidity or from fastidious pride. For love not only casts out fear, it also casts out the kind of false self respect that means refusing to get your hands dirty. Christ dined with tax-collectors and other riff-raff, but also with the establishment, the Pharisees. He talked theology with the Samaritan woman who was no better than she should be, but also with Nicodemus the 'master in Israel'.

All is not wrong with the Church. It never could be, and the reason why it is right to fight the evil in her is that she is Christ's Body, and a community of love. This isn't just a pious phrase, a 'beautiful construct'. It is as humanly evident as the corruption that shares its bed. It can be seen, heard, handled—as physically as people saw, heard and handled Christ, the Word of life. It is the same Word, it is being spoken now as much as ever, and in many ways louder than ever before. If the conflict is what catches the public eye, then that should be an opportunity to show also the reality of love. It's up to us.

This book arose out of gloom and anxiety. There was something like a war going on in the Church. It seemed all wrong. Something *must* be done. How could peace be restored? But you can't *restore* peace, it isn't something we build, it is the dynamic stillness we discover at the heart of living. And we discover this only in the communion of freedom, expressed in utter obedience to the Spirit in the Church.

I can't do better than use another quotation from Daniel Berrigan. It says the whole thing much better than I can—but I'm saying it, and I want to go on saying it, over and over again:

'A time of war judges the time of peace that has gone before, and the quality of those who built the peace. Were they truly peaceful men, or were they sunning themselves along a wall they had not helped to raise? To go along with such a peace is very like going along with war.

'The price of a false peace is as high as the price of a hot war. In fact, the cost of the first amounts to exactly the inevitability of the second.

'A time of division, of misunderstanding, and of friction may well seem the least auspicious time of healing or of reconciliation. And yet, when love is in question, the opposite may also be true. The worst of times may be the best of times.

'One must accept the ironies of life and take up the tasks of life. Disgraced or not, foolish or not, living in ill times or good, we are what we are, we are where we are. The actual world is our only world. We must go forward: we must accept all that men say of us, however painful or unfair it be. The times allow for no delay. Life grants us no space for idleness, regrets, the pursuit of illusions. The work of peace must go on, in hardiness and steadfast good humour. We must consent to being ourselves, to being unworthy vessels of God's word, to working with others, to the slow inching forward of compassion and hope.

'What is the task before us? It is as large as life itself
and remains so. Even when . . . we must take an unfre-
quented road, still our journey must not be solitary or
capricious. It must be a journey with men and for men. It
must form the largest possible company which is com-
mensurate with a good conscience. It must include men
who agree with us wholly, men who disagree in part, men
who confront us with unwelcome alternatives. All are our
brothers; it is their task as well as our own. We journey
towards man. We all hear the same cry in the darkness—
the wounded and the violated, the neglected poor, the
victims of our history, those in whose destruction we have
had part.'

The cry is always the same, it is to answer it that Christ
came, and sends us. The world lacks hope and we have it.
But if people are to listen to the message they must see that
we believe what we preach. That doesn't mean we have to
pretend everything's fine. It isn't. 'Not only creation, but we
ourselves, who have the first-fruits of the Spirit, groan
inwardly as we wait for the adoption of sons, the redemption
of our bodies. For in this hope we were saved.' The point is,
we don't even know what that hope means, we don't know—
can't know—what it is we hope for, yet we do hope. This
can draw people together, in spite of (or perhaps because of)
any amount of unrest and anxiety and disagreement, for 'we
know that in everything God works for good, with those who
love him'.

At this point I don't know what to say. This is a personal
letter, yet it isn't just that, because it is written to be read
by a great many people. Most of them I shall never meet. I
can't help wondering what they'll think. Will they feel: what
ridiculous arrogance, who does she think *she* is, saying all
those high-sounding things? Maybe they will, and they will

be right. Or at least they will be if I forget for one moment that I speak in the Church. It is that—and not any chance collection of qualities, or the bizarre circumstances that led me finally to tea in your study, and the plan of a book—that makes it possible and right for me to speak, and to speak with the voice of the Church. It is the Church's voice that speaks in those quotations from the exiled Jesuit, and from St Paul. But it is also the voice of the Church that speaks when it's just me, insofar as I try to speak with, in and through the Church. That doesn't mean that all I say is right, but that the Spirit in the Church helps me, and also helps others to hear, in what I say, whatever is good, and of the Spirit.

I don't think there is much more to say. In authority or under authority, we have to work together at a task that we can never finish because only God can finish it. It's more difficult now than ever before, because we are more than ever surrounded by incomprehension and suspicion (mostly through our own fault). The language of our preaching sounds like nonsense to most people—and in a sense it *is* nonsense, for 'it pleased God through the folly of what we preach to save those who believe'. But this nonsense, this foolishness, must not be the babble of a strange language but the challenge of a folly that can convert. It must preach in the language of action that speaks to people now. A language of authority, of obedience, and both at once, which is good Christian nonsense. Christ's authority, Christ's obedience. The authority of love and of service, the obedience of poverty and of death. Out of that comes new life. New life, perhaps, for the Church in England. We can't tell, all we can do is hope, and be ready to do whatever turns up to be done, and do it together.

When I began this second part of the book my head was full of bright ideas and suggestions. They seem to have evaporated, which is just as well because (even if these were all as brilliant as they momentarily seemed) they aren't what matters. What matters is to realize that we are all called, all consecrated, endowed with the Spirit, able to hear him and to speak his Word. Not for our individual selves, but because we are the Church. In that case, as St Paul might have put it nowadays:

'Who can separate us from the love of Christ? Can unrest, or anxiety, or persecution, or lack of funds, or of prestige, or the precariousness of our structures, or the threat of war?'

And the answer is clear:

'Neither the chances of death or life, nor occult messengers, nor dictators, nor the present trouble, nor future difficulties, nor mysterious powers (whether we think of them as out in space or in the depth of our own minds) nor, in fact, anything else in all creation, can possibly separate us from the love of God which comes to us in Christ Jesus our Lord.'

Four

Cardinal Heenan

My dear Rosemary,

We agreed to write this book within an hour of our first meeting. You have a husband and nine children. There are nearly a thousand priests and over half a million Catholics in my diocese. So it is hard to imagine two people more unlikely to be able to find time for authorship. Nevertheless we have somehow managed to write. I wonder if it will prove worthwhile? I don't know what you are going to say about my first piece. I imagine that you found a great deal in it to annoy you. As for your part I found nothing to be cross about but a great deal to wonder at. How differently each of us looks at people and they at us! They treat you in a special way because you are something of a phenomenon. You began to write fairly recently but already your name is well known to English-speaking Catholics throughout the world. It must be hard for you on your travels to engage in ordinary conversation. You refer to the people you meet at parent-teacher sessions, parish jumble sales and Newman lectures. Regarding them as a cross-section of the Catholic community you assume that the views they express are typical. You forget that it is to you they are talking. They are most unlikely to discuss similar topics or express the same views when you are not present. Being Rosemary Haughton cuts you off from quite a slice of reality.

Being a bishop cuts me off, of course, far more. To a limited extent even a priest is cut off but a bishop is almost blindfolded by his flock. When, for example, I go to see the sick and housebound, the day and time of my arrival is known well in advance. Relatives or neighbours make the house ready for my visit. I have been inside thousands of poor homes since I became a bishop in 1951 but I have rarely seen a dirty room. Fortunately the effects of episcopal consecration do not include amnesia. For most of the previous twenty-one years I had served in poor parishes. I knew every home and every family. To some extent, as I have just said, even a priest is out of touch. People are careful of their language and appearance when a priest calls. But once a priest is well known he becomes a member of every family and there is very little he does not know about his people. A bishop has an additional bar to reality because even his own priests will not always talk to him as they do to each other. They may not deliberately mislead him but for many good reasons they do not tell him all that is in their minds. After a frank and cordial talk with his priests a bishop cannot feel fully confident that he knows exactly what his clergy are thinking—especially about himself and the way he administers the diocese.

I do not therefore pretend that I am in a position to put you right about the outlook of priests and people. I think, however, that I can correct some of your impressions. When you have read what I have to say you may be unchanged or even confirmed in your views. That does not greatly matter since you will at least know that there is another side to consider. I do not, in fact, care very much if I fail to alter any of your ideas because, on the whole, I like them. You are not my problem. You, after all, came to me freely because you were worried. My problem are those who will not go to bishops or clergy when they are worried. My present problem are those who will read what I write only to find added justification for their hostility. They may accept nothing from a bishop but I hope they will learn something from you. At least you have shown that a stranger can come to her father in God and be received with compassion and affection.

There are those who will regard our collaboration as an act of betrayal on your part. They will think of you as advancing towards the hierarchy with a white flag. (How little they know you!) Yet it is important to consider them—although their number is not large—before embarking on any criticism of what you have written. This book is not intended only for them but also and especially for the many who feel estranged and unhappy. Their number is not small. They are not embittered but, on the contrary, eager to be reassured. They will be glad to see proof that the alleged civil war between educated laity and the shepherds of the flock is largely a private battle led by a few. The majority of educated Catholics take no part in public polemics. They are distressed by what they read and anguished by the picture of disunity so sedulously advertised. Some seek comfort from their priests while others write confidential letters to their bishops. It is they, more than any others, who will profit most from this book of ours. For the rest your example will help young people. They admire you and will follow you. They will learn that a Catholic can argue with a bishop and that such action is not servile but filial.

I enjoyed what you wrote and I agree with much of it. But your interpretation of facts is coloured by your limited acquaintance with run-of-the-mill Catholics. You have spent so much time with the disillusioned that you almost give the impression that they are the main body in the

Church. You accept their premises uncritically. 'Of course they were right' you say of those who were horrified that Pope John, 'a simple-minded idealist', had let loose a revolution. That is not, in fact, what horrified those opposed to the Council. It was not, as you suggest, that they feared that the Church would capitulate to the secular world. They feared that with so little preparation the Council would make the Church a laughing stock. 'Of course they were wrong' is what I would say—but they came very near to being proved right. The depression of the Fathers of the Council towards the end of the first session was equalled by that of Pope John. The Pope's depression was partly caused by the cancer that was killing him painfully. At the time of his death the Council was still a failure but, of course, it was only beginning. I do not share your belief that the bishops were afraid the Council would lead the faithful to ask too many questions and ultimately question the need for the Church's continued existence. This kind of speculation did not arise from the Council any more than the now celebrated 'Is God dead?' controversy did. It is a common confusion to attribute to the Council the theological theories current in Protestant circles. The Woolwich school of theology, for example, derives not from the Council in Rome but from Germany.

The things you say we hoped for when the Council started —a simpler liturgy, an up-to-date presentation of theology, closer ties with men of other faiths—are all being realized. I do not think that the Council is entirely responsible for the restlessness which exists among all who love the Church and who, irrespective of their standard of education, search for the message the Church is giving to the men of our time. But this restlessness is exaggerated by the disgruntled within the Church. Its main cause is probably lack of guidance on contraception. This I shall discuss in its place. You will see that it has very little to do with the Council itself. Another reason for discontent and bewilderment is the constant change in the manner of celebrating Mass. Everyone with pastoral experience knows the changes should have been introduced more gradually. Unfortunately the experts gathered in Rome have relatively few among their number who have been parish priests. Prudent delay is regarded as a betrayal. At home a pause before introducing the latest concession from Rome is likely to lead to letters in *The Times*. It is forgotten that not one Catholic in ten has any regular contact with the Church except at Sunday Mass. Ten per cent is a bold estimate if we include the many who attend Mass only occasionally. The majority of Catholics know of the Church only what they hear at Mass or read in their newspapers. They are therefore aware of only two developments. First, they see that the Mass, hitherto the one fixed event in their spiritual experience, is constantly changing. Secondly, the secular press has begun to publish Catholic news. It tends to concentrate on noisy exits of Catholic clergy and anything else however remotely touching sex and the Church. Restlessness about theology affects only an important minority. They will be the chief readers of our book but it is a gross error to confuse them with the main body of the faithful. I want to make this point very clearly because you tend to speak of the few as if they alone were significant.

It is not that I think numbers to be the test of pastoral need. It was probably an exaggeration to say, as St Francis de Sales is alleged to have said, that one soul is diocese enough for any bishop. But every group, however small or lowly, is the concern of the Church. You, I think, are unduly influenced by those who employ revolutionary language. Without accepting their jargon or their attitudes you are evidently impressed, for example, by what you call the *Slant* group. You think that it is 'basically part of something so deeply and importantly Christian that it is hard to recognize or accept just because it is so fundamental'. I agree that many in this group are earnest Christians who use Marxist terminology as General Booth impounded popular tunes for use with his hymns. But some are religious dilettantes. They have no good word for the Church and probably only a superficial knowledge of the Marxism they admire and advocate. They remind me of Lysenko, who sought to depose Mendel from the biologists' Olympus in favour of the Marxist Michurin. Lysenko held that biologists throughout the West clung to Mendelism only because of their senseless hostility to Marxist dogma. Only as recently as May 1966 did the Soviet scientists officially reject the Lysenko nonsense (their own word) in the scientific journal *Heredity*. Catholics who have studied the history of Marxism regard with alarm the attempt to interpret the teaching of Christ through an essentially atheistic philosophy. Those who contend that Marxism can be anything other than atheistic evidently think that the Marxist doctrine is to be found only in *Das Kapital*.

The tragedy of the 'Christian Leftists' you describe is that their powerful and authentic desire of reforming the Church is drained of love. They have declared war on the authorities in the Church and rejected the whole notion of dialogue (which is, of course, a form of Christian love). The unhappy outcome of the constant battering of the pastors of the flock is that whatever good things the critics have to say go largely unheard. Crude and repetitious attacks on bishops who, however mistaken, are doing what they believe to be right, angers Christian people. That is why I disagree with you when you say that the influence of the left wing is growing. I think, on the contrary, that while the group itself has become more bitter and intransigent the people they might have influenced have become bored. Their publicists have destroyed the prospect of progress by humourless and sometimes frenzied attacks on the Church as an institution. If they give the impression of hating the Church they will not make headway among those who love the Church. No word of praise or love of the Church escapes them. To destroy and tear down the Church as we know it is their declared intent. Of course the believers among them do not really mean all they say. Hence their failure. If they spoke with love their message might be heard and would be effective in removing abuses.

Their message, indeed, may be well worth hearing. They feel that it was mainly the hazards of history which led to the loss of evangelical simplicity. Emerging from imperial persecutions the Church suddenly found herself free and honoured. Christianity became the official religion and the Church assumed much of the glory of a declining Empire. It was natural for Christians to grasp the power and position so long denied them. The story of the growth of the Church's power would be incredible were it not for incontestable proofs of its truth. Constantine laid the foundations of the Church's temporal power. Before long the pope had become the most influential person in Europe. This influence was emerging even before Pippin had given the pope territory which virtually created the papal states. This was possibly the most notorious kiss of death in Christian history. Unhappily by the later middle ages the political power of the papacy frequently overshadowed its prime spiritual function. The cure of souls could be a lucrative profession while high ecclesiastical rank was often sought mainly for the wealth and prestige it brought.

The depravity of prelates was commonplace and excited little reaction until the revolt called the Reformation. It is true that scandal at the heart of Christendom had not always been accepted in silence by the articulate. Dante found suitable places for bishops in his inferno. Savonarola lashed the sinful shepherds and called down upon them the curse of

E

God. But it is also true that even in the worst days God raised up such holy Dominicans as Catherine of Siena and Vincent Ferrer to show that despite the corruption of its rulers the Church was still a nursery for saints. Once involved in worldly affairs, however, it was difficult for the Church to rid herself of material entanglements. Despite the spiritual renewal incidental in the Counter-Reformation, the Catholic Church, sometimes for better but often for worse, could not escape association with politics and the whole apparatus of the State. This is what many of the most ardent among modern reformers find intolerable.

Once the Church had become a great institution it was inevitable that she should have evolved a system of law. Even the Apostolic Church was an hierarchical institution but it was small in numbers and, following Christ's command, remained poor in spirit. Not for nothing, however, was the Church Roman. Soon *majestas* became one of her outstanding features. Persecution and prosperity alike ministered to her consciousness of being the Church of God. Gradually she came to regard herself as a strong fortress. She proudly claimed the four marks which distinguished her from all other institutions. The Church—the *ecclesia,* the gathering of God's people—was becoming less easily recognizable as Christ's 'little flock'.

After the Second Vatican Council *ecclesia semper reformanda* was adopted as a slogan. Many, moved by God's grace, humbly repeated it and searched their consciences to reform themselves as the first and essential step in the reformation of the Church. Others looked not at themselves but at their fellow members and the whole divine institution. To the Church herself rather than to its sinful members they addressed the words the Spirit spoke to the Bishop of Laodicea:

'You say to yourself "I am rich, I have made a fortune and have everything I want", never realizing that you are wretchedly and pitiably poor and blind and naked too. I warn you, buy from me the gold that has been tested in the fire to make you really rich, and white robes to clothe you and cover your shameful nakedness, and eye ointment to put on your eyes so that you are able to see' (Apoc. iii, 17–19).

The Council is the ointment given by the Spirit to the angels of modern Churches. We have begun to see that in his language riches are poverty and poverty riches. If we were ever to become lowly we needed first to be humiliated. Our defects are no longer hidden. They are broadcast even by the Church's own children. The children of Israel turned against Moses and this was for the ultimate good of the chosen people. Perhaps the frequent attacks on those in authority will purify them too. Although the Church is besought to ignore accepted social conventions it is not either practical or desirable for the Church to attempt to contract out of the modern world. She must not destroy what she holds in trust for the work God has called her to do.

The Church must constantly examine her motives for possessing any of the goods of this world and seek to detach herself more completely from the standards of the world. In company with all civilized people Christians have begun to see the scandal of riches in the midst of poverty. Before the Council the primacy of the right of private ownership was already yielding to the rights of the whole community. Each fresh pronouncement by the Church—especially the encyclical: *Justice and Peace (Populorum Progressio)*—underlines the Christian duty of sharing possessions. In this sense the 'Leftists' are serving the cause of Christ by calling for more detachment from the system of monopoly capitalism. Marxism, nevertheless, is not of God. For all their righteousness those Catholics who advocate it are obstructing true reform. Salvation comes from the gospel of Jesus Christ, not the Communist Manifesto.

You say that in the Church there is a feeling of disillusion which moderate Council enthusiasts suffer more than anyone since things have not worked out as they had hoped. As an indication of this you point out that people attend Benediction less frequently and, you add, 'they don't exactly flock to Mass in the evenings'. This is an excellent example of the distressing way in which the manner of implementing the Council's decrees is made responsible for everything that happens in the contemporary Church. It is invoked to justify every new theological theory and blamed for every blemish in the life of the Church. The decrees of the Council could be read in a single day but unfortunately many people read not the decrees themselves but only books and articles about the decrees. There might be less confusion if all Catholics were to read what the Council said of itself. This is not always the same as the accounts given by writers of popular theology. Thus you attribute decline of attendance at Benediction to disillusionment following the Council. In fact it has nothing whatever to do with the Council. The fall in attendance at evening devotions began with the blackout in the second world war. Attendance picked up for a few years after the war until television enticed congregations away. The *coup de grâce* was delivered by the introduction of evening Mass by Pope Pius XII. The disappearance of Benediction has nothing to do either with the Council or recent attacks on eucharistic doctrine. The pastoral life of the Church in this country has followed a fairly steady trend. The Council as yet has exerted relatively little influence. This will certainly come during the next decade.

You mention the fact that membership of Catholic organizations is diminishing and that young people are not joining. This is also true to some extent of the priesthood and the religious life. It is one of the signs of weakness in the Church of our day. It is unlikely that the organizations themselves are entirely to blame if recruits fail to offer themselves. The most nearly perfect organization for Catholic men is the Society of St Vincent de Paul. Without publicity of any kind members visit the poor, the sick, the old and the imprisoned. They bring relief to body and mind. They are at the service of the bereaved, the distressed and all who need help with their social or domestic problems. Some of our finest professional men are active members. Among such as these you will find few critics of the Church. If the ranks of such organizations are thin either God is not calling or man is not responding. It is possible that the young men of the type which used to join the Society of St Vincent de Paul or enter seminaries and novitiates are so busy discussing what is wrong with the Church that they do not hear God's voice inviting them to surrender to his love. Catholic students can be suffocated by too frequent attendance at conferences. Those who continually criticize the Church to the young bear a great responsibility. The occasional silence of a retreat might enable the voice of the Spirit to be heard. Some would be told: 'Go sell all thou hast and give to the poor and come follow me' (Matt. xix, 21). When the stream of converts and of vocations ceases to flow it is a sign that all is not well with the Church. Happily after an alarming drying up the stream seems now to be flowing once more.

Since the Council our young people have not always been well served. Nobody expects boys and girls of nineteen or twenty to be profound thinkers. It is unfair to feed their minds with an exclusive diet of the new Catholic jargon. Long before middle age they will have repudiated this dismal jargon—which, in any case, by then will be out of date—but they may have lost the faith in the process. When words are offered in place of ideas young people are defrauded. To breed cynicism about the Church is as bad as the old fault of pretending that nothing could ever be wrong. In our complacency we used to talk as if each Catholic personally possessed the four marks of the Church. This must often have made us insufferable to other Christians. Unconsciously we must have been conceited as we regarded with pity the unfortunates with no infallible voice to guide them. Looking back we may well be ashamed of the near-scorn we felt for religious denominations in which no recognizable authority could be discerned. This regrettable attitude is remembered by those who now seek to disturb the complacency of young Catholics. But that is no reason why we should teach them to scoff at the magisterium of the Church and talk in rollicking contempt of all the theology of yesterday.

You rightly say that the birth control issue has undermined the confidence of many Catholics. You suggest that one of the most harmful results is that different priests give contradictory advice to their penitents. The result is that in some places the couples practising contraception may be receiving the sacraments in good conscience while in a neighbouring parish contracepting couples are regretfully abstaining. This problem comes only indirectly from the Council. For many years there has been widespread discussion about the morality of contraception. Even had there been no pronouncement by the Lambeth Conference supporting contraception, it is probable that Pope Pius XI would still have written his encyclical. It must not be forgotten that the encyclical *Casti Connubii* was considered by nobody at the time of its publication to contain new teaching. It was universally accepted as a clear statement of the traditional moral doctrine of the Church. This does not mean that all Catholics received the Pope's words with joy. Many even then thought the doctrine too hard to follow. Only a few left the Church, though many while remaining faithful to the Mass now began to abstain from the sacraments. Others despite frequent falls continued to frequent the sacraments to gain grace and strength to obey. As always there were not lacking those who said that a celibate clergy cannot understand the problems of married people. Despite *Casti Connubii* some still felt justified in receiving Holy Communion while continuing to use contraceptives. Most Catholics at that time agreed that only normal intercourse is licit and that family limitation should be achieved by self-denial. Some Catholics, on the other hand, allege that calculated love-making is a travesty of true love. There is clearly a wide difference both in conviction and practice. It is impossible in such an intimate matter to know exactly what proportion of Catholics conform to the Pope's teaching. Estimates of what percentage of Catholics practises contraception are unreliable even when they are called sociological surveys.

A doctrine may be hard, but if it is God's truth it must be accepted. This was the universal Catholic outlook until the truth of the Church's teaching was publicly questioned in the Council. The whole Catholic world was thrown into confusion by two or three speeches. If a bishop could question the accepted view of contraception perhaps the teaching of the Church needed to be re-examined. The astonishment of the Fathers on hearing an attack on the teaching of *Casti Connubii* was considerable. Nobody therefore was surprised when the Pope hurriedly withdrew contraception from public debate. This was obviously a wise decision. Delicate issues affecting the consciences of millions should never have been broached in a company of thousands. When the full history of the Second Vatican Council is written it may be revealed that a few days earlier one hierarchy, foreseeing this very danger, had sent a memorandum to the Pope requesting that this subject should be debated not publicly in St Peter's but at private meetings of national hierarchies. The results of these discussions were then to be given to the Holy Father for consideration and action. Perhaps it is unfortunate that this proposal was not found acceptable.

Had there been a thorough examination of the question by the whole body of bishops meeting in private it might have been possible to have given the Pope a comprehensive account of the state of opinion within the Church before the end of the Council. There might not have been the agonizing delay which has proved so harmful to the authority of the Holy See. Immediately after the Council a commission of theologians, doctors, scientists, demographers and economists, together with some married couples, was set up to consider the whole question and advise the Pope. Not surprisingly it could reach no unanimous decisions. At one time the Pope appeared to become impatient. Addressing members of the pontifical commission in audience he begged them to make more haste. But haste is not always possible in a search for truth. If some members regarded contraceptives as offensive both morally and aesthetically while others held that, however unattractive, contraceptives have now become virtually essential to the harmony of married life, there was no way of hastening the commission's decision. No doubt the economists and demographers were able to show the need for family planning—which nobody doubts or doubted—but their qualifications did not enable them to decide whether or not artificial contraception is sinful. Ultimately this remains a theological question. The papal pronouncement when it comes must take into consideration both the principles of moral theology and the testimony of Catholic wives and husbands. Given the variety of views it is not surprising that Pope Paul has taken so long to issue his promised statement.

It is not likely that medical and scientific knowledge will greatly assist the Pope in arriving at the decision he has undertaken to make. The press from the beginning seemed to assume that this array of scientific talent was assembled in order to study the morality of contraceptive pills. According to some papers the commission was asked to consider the possibility of producing a 'Catholic' pill. The proceedings of the pontifical commission were secret but there was little reason to hope that they would remain so. Despite an oath of secrecy a version of the commission's findings has appeared in the French press, the *National Catholic Reporter*, a Catholic newspaper run by laymen in America, and in the London *Tablet*. If there is ever to be a truly confidential commission to advise the Pope, there will have to be a much clearer understanding of the solemn nature of an oath of secrecy. Once any disclosure has been made, a commission is at the mercy of commentators. Members who respect their oath will not feel themselves at liberty to correct, explain, confirm or deny the version of proceedings which has been made public.

The press is never slow to produce a theory to fit alleged facts. Thus, for example, the press told the world that following the final meeting of the pontifical commission the 'progressive' Cardinal Doepfner of Munich took the report to the Holy Father. The explanation given was that the 'reactionary' Cardinal Ottaviani had refused to take the report to the Pope. The truth is less exciting. Cardinal Ottaviani was President of the pontifical commission *ex officio* as Prefect of the Congregation for the Teaching of the Faith. The Cardinal is nearly blind and finds difficulty in conducting a meeting. The Holy Father therefore appointed Cardinal Doepfner and myself pro-Presidents. We shared the oversight of the meetings. When all was over Cardinal Ottaviani, who had presided only formally, asked me as pro-President to present the report to the Pope. But since I had to return at once to Westminister, Cardinal Doepfner kindly agreed to stay behind while the report was being retyped. That is how he came to present the report. Details of this kind are unimportant in themselves but they show with what caution reports of confidential matters should be received. You are right in saying that until the Pope speaks any pronouncement on the subject by lesser authorities must be so carefully worded as virtually to say nothing—or, at least, nothing new. I doubt if the Holy Father foresaw how long it would take before he could conscientiously make a full statement on contraception. We may thank God that even the abuse of some of his own sons did not precipitate a pronouncement on a question of such importance to the faithful.

It is embarrassing and painful for those in authority to be able to give so little guidance. It is easy for those without responsibility to attack the Pope's attitude and, indeed, it has become popular to do so. There is no doubt, as the Pope has said, about the Church's teaching. Even those outside the Church know the current Catholic teaching on contraception, abortion and divorce. But while there is no doubt about her teaching there are grounds for saying that circumstances have changed so much—the status of women, for example, and the notion of love in marriage—that the relevance of the traditional language may be questioned. Even the words 'contraception' and 'birth control' have undergone changes of meaning in our own time. It is clear that a restatement of Catholic teaching is urgently needed. This does not mean that the Church now doubts the validity of the moral principles upon which her teaching has been based. An example from a different field may illustrate this point. The Church, let us suppose, was right though not infallible in decreeing the invalidity of Anglican orders. This, however, has not prevented English bishops from assuring Pope Paul that there would be no objection from Catholics if the whole question were to be re-examined. Much has happened since the time of Pope Leo XIII. There has been much greater inter-communion between Anglicans and the Orthodox. The validity of Orthodox orders has never been in question. That is only one aspect of Anglican orders which might now be re-examined with profit. It would have to be made clear, of course, that to reopen the question would not indicate doubt about the original decision, which rested largely upon the inadequacy of the sacramental form. Possibly the same verdict would be returned today. In this, as in the question of contraception, the Church must show herself ready to examine new evidence. Nevertheless it is true that until the promised pronouncement of the Pope on birth control the Church will continue to be restless and troubled.

I want to look at the Catholic world you inhabit. It is full of disillusioned priests, religious and laity. You travel the country and find everywhere a sense of isolation, frustration and hopelessness. The reason, you say, is the lack of any feeling that what is being achieved is recognized as significant by the official leaders of the Church. Let me speak very frankly. It is not my experience that those who are busy about God's work have a sense of isolation, hopelessness and frustration. There is too much self-pity, too much talking and far too much self-imposed isolation among the groups of which you speak. To talk, as you do, of lack of contact among those doing pioneering work is really to say that many of them ignore the existing organizations in the Church. Whatever might happen if dioceses, parishes and Catholic schools were to be abolished, at present the lay apostolate must be carried out with bishops and parish priests as fathers and brothers in a united Christian community. Those who avoid their clergy disregard the whole spirit of the Council. It simply is not true to say that bishops and clergy impede the work of pioneers. Many laymen who might be doing good work for God are dissipating their energies in endless discussions instead of putting themselves to work under the direction of pastoral priests. That is plain speaking but without it there can be no true dialogue between us. I do not speak with indignation but with compassion for those who suffer frustration.

Your words about young priests made me realize the unreality of the Church you describe. You picture the young priest heroically struggling to do his pastoral work without rebelling at the restrictions, indifference and criticism of his superiors. Apparently all goes well for years. He does not express grievances because he is primarily interested not in himself but in his work. You say that one must know such people personally to realize the extent of their suffering. This picture saddens me because it shows how difficult it is even for zealous laity to know what priests are really like. I doubt if many young priests today have to withstand a tithe of the frustrations endured by young priests thirty or forty years ago. Curate-killing superiors are largely relics of a past age. The priest of today usually has only himself to blame if he is not able to do God's work. Never was it more easy for a priest to see and speak to his bishop. Your army of disillusioned clerics does not exist. Isolate a couple of priests and, of course, they will be ready to grumble and talk gloomily about their work and their superiors. We have all, in our time, done the same. You say that any prolonged discussion in a sympathetic group reveals in young priests a deep frustration often leading to rooted bitterness and cynicism. I doubt if there is any happier group of men in the world than busy pastors of souls. A 'sympathetic' group may create grievances of which the young priest was hitherto unaware.

That is part of the explanation. 'Prolonged discussions' can be the cause of much misery. You must ask yourself what result is expected from these discussions. They are rarely exercises in self-criticism. From experience I know that it is rarely profitable to spend hours revealing deep frustrations to any group, however sympathetic. Our deep frustrations by definition are always caused by somebody else. My frustrations would be caused by the Pope, my fellow bishops or my clergy and faithful. They could never be caused by myself. When I was younger and valued time less, I spent hours discussing my frustrations in sympathetic groups. I criticized my bishop, my parish priest, my fellow curates, my parishioners. When I grew older I realized that much apparent frustration is self-imposed. There is always an outlet for souls in love with Christ. The saints were cheerful because they worked and prayed. There is far too much foolish talking among the under-employed. If dialogue means anything, the frustrated priests of your acquaintance should talk to their superiors and either reach an understanding or ask for a change of work. But their chief dialogue should be with God. That is the most neglected dialogue of all. The Blessed Trinity is the most sympathetic group in existence.

You say a great deal about love, but not nearly enough. Love is too often used as a catch-phrase. Christian love is far removed from the sentimental sort of love of which most people talk. Christian love is a disciplined love and almost always involves suffering. The strict mother who refuses to let her children stay up late watching television is showing Christian love. But the slovenly woman who lets her children do what they like may be regarded as the more loving mother by her neighbours. Since the Council there has been too much talk about loving, but too little love. The priest, nun or layman who lovingly serves the sick and the poor is too tired to keep talking about love. Those who for the love of Christ work really hard have little energy left for making speeches about love. Their whole life, like that of most mothers, is a prolonged act of love. Suspect those who talk constantly of love. Love, like freedom, is easily prostituted. Since the Council there have been many attacks made on the Church by men with love on their lips and hatred in their hearts.

Love is not a one-way street. Priests love their people and people their priests. Similarly there is a genuine affection and respect between bishops and priests. There is nothing quite comparable among religious because superiors normally have short periods of office. This may give too little time for developing the relationship of father and sons. At ordination the priest is asked to pledge reverence and obedience to his bishop. He replies: 'I promise' and the bishop gives him a kiss. The obedience of diocesan priests is exemplary. Rarely does a priest refuse his bishop's request. The bishop, in turn, will meet the wishes of his priests unless there is some strong reason for refusing. Bishops and priests are bound together by a common desire to serve their people. As in all families there are disagreements and, perhaps, moments of anger. Love is one of the characteristics of the Church and it often astonishes outsiders when they first see priests and people together. Those who say that there is no love within the Church may have too little love in their own hearts.

You tend to dramatize the weakness of the Church as a human community. There are, of course, unimaginative and unloving superiors. But most of them are kindly, zealous, intelligent men and women anxious only to do God's work well. It is not true that most of their subjects want to work but are prevented from doing so. Most of us who are placed

in positions of authority rejoice when we find people—
priests, religious or laymen—with initiative and a desire for
action. It has not been my experience that those in authority
only obstruct and discourage. Usually superiors are scrupulous about not interfering with those in charge of a project.
They cannot accept every scheme proposed to them but intelligent people do not interpret every refusal as a rebuff.
Disapproval and discouragement are accorded to certain
proposals mainly because they would not further God's work.
Superiors do not say 'No' because it has a more attractive
sound than 'Yes'.

Coming up against final opposition, you say, some people
leave the Church because the reform they are working for
seems more vital than the reasons given for preventing it.
The Council encouraged people to explore but, you say, they
soon clash with those in authority who are generally repres-
sive. An organization, you suggest, that can so frustrate a
genuine desire for truth and community no longer seems to be
a credible witness to Christ. Without pretending fully to
understand your argument (largely because the words 'community' and 'credible' in your context are not clear to me) I
can only say that frustration caused by those in authority
cannot justify any of us in rejecting the Church of Christ.
Like yourself, I would not dare to judge the conscience and
motive of individuals. Very long experience, however, has
led me to observe certain common characteristics among
those who leave the Church. The first is failure to pray. There
is much talk about prayer. But, as with love, there is more
talk than action. Since the Council some have in practice
abandoned prayer in the sacred name of liturgy. Forsaking
prayer led to the downfall of the Jewish people, but this is
not given a sufficiently prominent place in the teaching of
salvation history. Without personal prayer men soon cease
to speak or listen to God. Without prayer nobody can keep a

humble and contrite heart which alone is acceptable to God. 'This people draw near with their mouth and honour me with their lips, while their hearts are far from me' (Isaiah xxix, 13).

With lack of prayer goes increase of self-esteem. If humility is the foundation of Christian virtue, pride is the first of the capital sins. We have no right to sit in judgement on the Church of God. We rarely have the right to sit in judgement on fellow members of the Church, for we are all sinful and ignorant. Nevertheless there can be occasions when we have the right to disagree with the words or actions of a person in authority—not excluding the pope himself. But disapproval of the Vicar of Christ is no justification for rejecting the Church of Christ. It is disingenuous for Catholics to justify their defection on grounds of disagreement with the views of the pope or the attitude of a bench of bishops. Educated Catholics will know of many scandals in the Church's long history. But I doubt if there has been a more zealous clergy and people in the Church at any time during the last thousand years. The Church is in a healthy state but it will not flourish if even in the name of liturgy we abandon personal prayer. There are communities today which in the flush of the liturgical revival concelebrate Mass without previous prayer or subsequent thanksgiving. If members of religious communities—preachers, retreat-givers and guides of youth—forsake prayer, the faithful will be spiritually starved. Priests and people faithful to prayer remain faithful to the Church of God.

The majority of the disgruntled, as you say, do not leave the Church. They stay and fight. You do not specify the enemies but it seems clear from the context that you mean the bishops. I question the need for fighting. The assumption appears to be that only a few laymen and religious see the true vision of the Church projected by the Council. When this vision is blocked they become angry because they assume that all opposition is the result of stupidity, dishonesty or timidity. This is surely a dangerous and uncharitable assumption. Uncharitable in this context means unloving. Why should the bishops who attended every session of the Council be ignorant of the Council's vision of the Church? Is it likely that those who have given their whole lives to the Church would suddenly wish to withstand its onward march? In any other social activity would it be taken for granted that only the amateurs are right? People easily come to regard themselves as theologians but the care of souls, according to St Gregory in his *Regula Pastoralis*, is the art of arts. It is splendid when scientists, historians, lawyers and doctors read books on theology, but this does not make them better qualified than bishops to make pastoral decisions. The matters most in dispute concern not speculative theology but pastoral care. It is in order for any Catholic or group of Catholics to request and even to campaign for fresh reforms. What is unwarranted is the assumption that any group of the laity is better informed and more concerned for the salvation of souls than the bishops. It is a wise rule to respect men's competence in the activity for which they have been trained. This is well understood in the university world.

Your picture of the critics of the hierarchy is scarcely recognizable. You say that they first demand reforms and only when these are refused do they write to the papers. If this were true it is unlikely that there would be any dispute between them and their bishops. Unhappily they rarely approach bishops before publicly attacking them. That, dear Rosemary, is the chief difference between them and you. Instead of denouncing me you came to see me.

Disloyalty towards the Church is a new feature in the Catholic life of this country. Within a family most disagreements can be calmly discussed but there has appeared in our community a group which specializes in public recrimination. This is a matter of grief to the bishops and of disedification to most educated laity. We have reached an odd state in which press attacks on pope, bishops or clergy are made almost exclusively by Catholics. A man's enemies are truly those of his own household. Owing to the influence of Pope John and the growth of ecumenism, those outside now usually refrain from criticizing the Church. In our trials they offer us only compassion. Time was when we used to express sympathy to our friends in the Church of England on their humiliations at the hands of publicity-seeking rebels. It is now their turn to sympathize.

It is, as I have said, rare for angry critics to make an approach to their bishops before denouncing them in the press. This is a pity because it would be improper for bishops to use the secular press for controversy with their own laity. It would be excusable for the faithful to complain to the press if they had no other channel to their fathers in God. But, in fact, bishops readily make themselves available. Nobody needing to see the bishop is likely to be refused an appointment. A great part of a bishop's time is devoted to receiving his priests and people. Members of other faiths are likewise invariably given a welcome. It is therefore unjust as well as unfilial for a Catholic to make public complaints before giving a bishop the opportunity of dealing privately with a grievance. Within the Catholic family there should be the same loving relationship as in any other family. This new spectacle of calculated uncharitableness towards those in authority is the more regrettable because it makes mockery of what the kindly Pope John tried to do.

I disagree with your notion of the kind of person who makes up the 'simple' faithful. My simple faithful are men and women of all standards of education who love the Church and are troubled by the present turmoil. They would be indignant to be told that they need to be protected by those you describe as the better informed Catholics. You unwittingly offend simple laity by suggesting that they need to be protected from their clergy by other laity. Your assertion that priests deliberately withhold information or fob them off with cheerful explanations and soft soap is a little unfair to the clergy. If you could put yourself in the place of pastors of souls you would realize why they think it wrong to introduce controversy into their sermons and instructions. No section of the clergy wishes to blindfold the laity or hide from them the decisions of the Council. It is not deceit which makes them refrain from preaching the latest theological theories. Remember that however popular it may become, a theory still remains a theory. Those who read theology will discuss far into the night the merits of every new theory (insight) but the simple faithful are more interested in actual doctrine. This is not denied them. Remember that what passes for new theology is sometimes only a rehash of old rationalism.

Theological controversy is excellent because it is the sign of life. If nobody were interested there would be no arguments. Throughout the history of the Church controversies have arisen to disturb scholars and, especially in the early centuries, to threaten the faith itself. Arians, Nestorians, Monophysites, Monothelites and Pelagians felt so strongly about their theories that they left the Church to found new sects.

There have been other lively controversies which did not involve heresy despite the hard words and accusations passing between the protagonists. It is some consolation at a time of violent disagreement within the fold to recall the even more bitter divisions of other days. The celebrated dispute between Jesuits and Dominicans on the question of grace and free will is an example. We can look back today with amusement to this quarrel, but it shook the Church in the sixteenth century and destroyed the peace of mind of many theologians as well as simple faithful. It was not only a battle of scholars. Writing to Pope Clement VIII from Spain Cardinal de Castro described the mischief:

'It is full of danger, for two religious orders of great renown are in conflict on the gravest of questions, a question that bears on the integrity of the faith. And this battle is carried on in public, in sermons and lectures. All sorts of people are mixed up in it, both learned and ignorant.'

The Pope announced that the whole question would be taken over by the supreme tribunal of the Church. All discussion of the question both private and public must cease. In due course Pope Clement set up the famous *Congregation de Auxiliis*, though he did not live to hear its verdict. It was what we would now call a pontifical commission.

History has its lessons for us today. It would be wrong for pastors of souls to become partisans in the many controversies which have arisen since the Council. It must be stressed that these do not concern the conciliar decrees themselves nor even their interpretation. Original sin, the Eucharist and the virginity of our Lady were not considered by the Council. By the next generation the current disputes will no doubt have given place to others. If priests were neglecting to instruct their people about the great renewal in the Church, the reform of the liturgy, the lay apostolate and all the other documents of the Council they would merit condemnation. But it is unfair to censure those wise priests who refuse to preach about questions in dispute. Time will show how many of the new theories are genuine advances in the Church's thinking. Meanwhile experienced pastors of souls study the views of theologians while giving their people only the doctrine of the Church.

I wonder if your analogy of disputes between parents is fully relevant. You rightly say that children are aware when all is not well between father and mother. They suffer from being shut out since they are quite capable of carrying undismayed the burden of an appalling family situation—provided they are trusted. I think it depends very much upon the nature of the family dispute. It also depends on the age and temperament of the children. If they are old enough to understand it is obviously wise to explain the troubles which arise from sickness and economic stress. Then, as you suggest, human love and heroism will triumph. Children will make sacrifices and display understanding and compassion until the crisis has passed. But there are other family situations which wise parents do not disclose to their children. The worst tragedies are often overcome precisely through the parents' determination not to shock or hurt the children. It would be foolish to stretch this analogy too far, but within the Church wise pastors do not disturb the theologically immature by retailing every controversy. Most Catholics, even the well educated, remain relatively ignorant of theology. It would be wrong to treat the faithful like children but it would also be wrong to confuse them needlessly. We hear much today about the false sense of security which Catholics are said to have too long enjoyed. Perhaps not enough is heard of the true sense of security to which, as members of the Church to which God's guidance has been promised until the end of time, they are entitled.

You speak of the illusion and uncertainty at all levels of Catholic life. I question the phrase 'at all levels'. If you were to say 'at most levels among academics' I would be more inclined to agree. But even here we must not be too sweeping. There are many literate Catholics abreast of the controversies within the Church who, far from being disturbed, are exhilarated by all that is happening in the theological field. Strong in faith they have no doubt that God is guiding his Church. Such men and women do not allow their spiritual lives to be upset by every new theological speculation. These are often genuine intellectuals and are aware of what scholars have said during earlier controversies. We must sympathize with young undergraduates who sometimes have the misfortune to be fed with speculative theology before they have had the opportunity to become acquainted with solid theology. They are offered cocktails while still needing the milk of doctrine. Naturally they become lightheaded. If their faith is undermined the responsibility must be borne largely by those whose prestige in other disciplines lends an illusion of authority to their theological speculations. It is still a virtue to feel with the Church (*sentire cum ecclesia*).

All this has to be pondered before writing off the whole Church of God as disillusioned and uncertain. Apart from the problem of contraception and the constant liturgical changes, I do not think that what is happening in the Church has affected more than a very small minority of the faithful. If you constantly meet only this minority it is possible to form a false impression. If, for example, you lived in North London you might think that a third of the nation's children are coloured. You might wonder why sermons are not constantly preached about racial problems. In other words, we need to see the whole picture before making universal judgements. A bishop on pastoral visitations sees different sections of his flock two or three times every week. He learns to allow for the dust thrown in his eyes and is in the best possible position to judge the extent of the unrest among active Catholics. People often don't know they are disillusioned until they are persuaded by the unhappy and disturbed. Not a few pencils are sharpened with the precise object of making

Catholics miserable in this post-conciliar phase in the life of the Church.

What you have to say about the nature of authority is, in my truly humble judgement, plausible and attractive but philosophically false. I may easily have misjudged you but as I read your words I was reminded of Rousseau's *Social Contract*. Your ideas on authority are certainly contemporary but not especially Christian. Like it or not, the authority our Lord spoke of was primarily power to be exercised: 'All authority in heaven and earth has been given to me' (Matt. xxviii, 18). That is the version given in the Jerusalem Bible. The Authorised and every other version read not 'all authority' but 'all power'. Etymology, of course, is not always a safe guide in seeking definitions. So while it is true that the word 'authority' derives from 'author' and that we talk of an author as an authority on his own subject, authority nevertheless means the possession and (usually) the exercise of real power. It would be pleasant to think of power as something completely unobtrusive but it would not be the kind of power Christ gave to his Church. The exercise of power is unobtrusive or not according to the personal qualities of those who exercise it. The greater and more self-evident the authority the less it needs to be asserted. The authority of a monitor in a primary school is in greater need of backing than that of a high court judge. But authority essentially means ruling—whether by local, national or ecclesiastical bodies.

You appear to suggest that the nature of authority in the Church is fortuitous. You describe it as a product of the feudal system. It seems clear that for you those in authority in the Church are vicegerents of the community. They are, in fact, vicegerents of Christ. The hierarchical nature of authority in the Church is not a haphazard growth. It is of divine origin. Similarly parental authority is not just a convenient form of family government but a natural, that is, a divine institution. The house of God has Christ as its corner stone and the apostles and first preachers (prophets) as its foundation. It was to the apostles that Christ gave the authority to preach and rule. The seventy-two disciples were sent out by Christ to act in his name. Their authority came from him and they were identified with him. 'Anyone who listens to you, listens to me: anyone who rejects you rejects me, and those who reject me reject the one who sent me' (Luke x, 16).

It is important to see what is meant by the crisis of authority. You say that the crisis is not about authority itself but about the language used by authority. The crisis, in your view, lies in the search for the proper way in which authority can be exercised today. This is loose thinking. The crisis is very real and it is a crisis less of exercising than of acknowledging authority. More simply it is, I think, a crisis of obedience. This becomes clear when we look at the disarray in certain communities bound by vows of poverty, chastity and obedience. Religious of the last generation may have taken their vow of poverty too literally. They were sometimes scrupulous and perhaps childish in their interpretation of obedience. They had to ask for their exact bus fare or the price of a meal each time they left their monasteries. The vow of poverty was a great cross for scholars who could not persuade hard-headed procurators that the latest books were essential for their studies. The spirit of poverty meant the re-use of old envelopes, patched clothing and a frugal use of light and heat. Modern conditions have made such observance of poverty more difficult. It is now regarded both as undignified and a waste of time to make constant recourse to superiors. St Francis of Assisi or, indeed, Fr Vincent

McNabb practised poverty in a manner which modern friars may be excused for regarding as an affectation.

The whole notion of obedience in some religious congregations has undergone a greater and more spiritually significant change. Community-room lawyers have pointed out that since every human act must be rational, no order should be obeyed unless and until it is seen to be wise. Obedience must yield place to dialogue. This, of course, is a long way from biblical theology. Abraham, Isaac, Jacob, Samuel and the other Old Testament heroes obeyed first and asked questions afterwards. Religious used to bind themselves by vow to obey their superiors in everything save sin. This ideal is now ridiculed by so many priests that not surprisingly their Sisters in religion and the laity are tempted to repudiate obedience. Weak superiors invariably court popularity. Pathetically they want to be well thought of and forget that those who follow Christ must accept the burden of responsibility even at the cost of popularity. As children we liked the masters who let us do as we liked. But it was not because of them that the school prospered. No institution thrives unless those in authority are prepared to rule.

You say that government is a function of authority but is not of its nature. I doubt if this is true. Government, in my view, is of the essence of authority and one of the chief causes of the crisis in the Church is the flouting of this aspect of authority. To put it more exactly it is not enlightened obedience but conceit which refuses to acknowledge the right of another to be in command. You will have noticed the critical attitude of certain priests towards their superiors and the selectivity with which pronouncements of the Pope or Council are received. A superior may make wrong decisions but he must never abdicate his responsibility. President Truman is said to have put a notice over his desk which read:

'The buck stops here.' The same might well be written over the desk of everyone in authority. Consultation and prayer should precede every big decision but it is wrong to suggest that the whole structure of authority in the Church has served its term and should now be discarded. The manner of exercising authority has changed. It has become more civilized and rational—not least because the standard of education has risen and orders can more easily be explained and understood. But unhappily some Catholics are no longer willing to acknowledge anyone holding authority in the Church as a person to whom obedience and respect are due. This attitude has led some to ask this kind of question: 'What function has a priest in the modern world? Does the Church now need religious orders? Cannot the lay people of God take over the activities of clergy and religious? Are we not all priests now? Do priestly powers really matter if the eucharistic elements do not change? Do we any longer need to confess our sins to a priest?'

There can be no doubt that some actually foster the crisis of authority. They talk of the Council but are blind to many of its decrees. Nobody who has studied what the Council laid down about the priesthood and the religious life has any excuse for a contemptuous attitude towards those consecrated to God. You say that authority is the community's reference to its source and that the arrangement of practical authority in the Church is 'likely to be' connected with the function of presiding at the Eucharist. You go on to say that abbots often had greater authority than bishops. But surely this is a different kind of authority. Monks need not be priests—it is doubtful if St Benedict himself was ever ordained. You appear to hold that authority resides in the community (the *Social Contract* once again) but this is not the teaching of the Church. We have to accept the Church as Christ founded it. In fact he made it hierarchical and, indeed, with due respect for the notion of collegiality, monarchical. It is tempting in these egalitarian days to dissimulate when we discuss the nature of the Church. The emancipated laity may call the priest 'brother' instead of 'father' and encourage him to put on lay clothes and go drinking with them. The immature priest may be flattered by this approach but it is contrary to the teaching of the Council on the priesthood. The priest, the Decree on the Priestly Ministry and Life says, must be a man set apart. Of course he should relax and, above all, be on affectionate and brotherly terms with those for whom he is pastorally responsible. But to regard the priest as having no different character and authority from a layman is not Catholic theology. It is doubtful, in fact, whether priests in lay clothes deceive the laity and enhance their pastoral influence.

You nowhere mention the magisterium which is the chief sign of authority in the Church of Christ. It is this authority which attracted Newman and, since his day, thousands of converts. The magisterium of the Church can be exercised by wise or foolish men. It can be narrow, brutal, or enlightened. It has been frequently abused and made an instrument of tyranny. But, to quote the old legal tag, *usum non tollit abusus*. The misuse of the magisterium does not destroy its proper function. It goes against liberal ideas to admit that those placed in authority have the right and duty to teach and rule. It is easy to see that the Index is an anachronism. It has been more or less a dead letter for many years. It is quite another matter to discard all censorship. The faithful have a right to be told if books are likely to be dangerous to their faith. There are many intelligent Catholics of good education who still expect the Church to guide them. An *imprimatur* does not guarantee that a book is worth reading but it does signify that a reputable theologian having read it considers that it does not threaten faith or morals. A humble Catholic does not accuse the Church of paternalism for protecting the non-theological from harmful reading. Not all paternal action is paternalistic. A wise parent exercises censorship over the reading of growing sons and daughters. To describe such action as paternalistic is to degrade true fatherhood.

Only anarchists believe that all government should be abolished. Even they eventually set up some form of government—usually dictatorial—when they have overthrown the existing government. Some modern Catholics are willing to acknowledge no rules beyond those of their own choosing. In so far as they conduct their whole religious life according to their own private interpretation they are rationalist. Essentially, however, they are anarchists. This can never become an option for followers of Christ 'who was made obedient unto death'. You say that the present crisis is due to a conflict between different notions of how authority should work. It is for you almost a question of semantics—the language of authority. This is much too flattering to those in revolt. While people are merely objecting to the uncompassionate or stupid acts and attitudes of those in authority they are spiritually safe. They may even be heroic in resisting those in power. But this is quite different from accepting the authority of pope, Council, bishop or priest only when it agrees with one's private judgement. The crisis of authority arises chiefly from the refusal of some modern disciples of Christ to listen to those whose responsibility it is to speak in the name of Christ.

People need to be ruled. That is the ethical justification for the existence of the State. Individuals and families do not possess the knowledge required to make decisions necessary for the good of the whole community nor the means to carry them out. Personally I am not capable of deciding such issues as comprehensive education, the building of the super-sonic Concord, the nationalization of steel or the British entry to the European Common Market. I have neither the time nor training to acquire knowledge of all the facts relevant to such policy making. If I had to find out everything for myself before civic action could be taken, the country could not be ruled. Citizens of the City of God are in just as much need of ruling as citizens in the State. If we had been left to make our own research few of us would have been able to discover the true faith which by God's grace is ours. Let me make it clear that I do not contend that Catholics have no right to criticize the decisions of authority. My point is that for the first time since the Reformation groups of Catholics are questioning the right of the Church to make any decisions at all. The controversy over contraception may be partly to blame for the crisis of authority. But only partly. Some Catholics today are simply unwilling to accept the magis-terium of the Church. I believe this to be a fundamental cause of the present crisis.

I agree with all you say about poverty but the problem of practising poverty in the way best suited to the relief of the destitute is much more complex than you imply. Voluntary poverty is obviously much easier to practise than the poverty imposed by circumstances. The Benedictine monk, for example, and the Carmelite nun take a vow of poverty, but life is much easier for them than for a starving family in Asia. Should they sell their monastery or convent in England and go to live in an Indian village? It can be argued that by selling all property the Church would become more Christ-like. If we were rid of our churches, schools, libraries and hospitals we would clearly be more free. But might we not be robbing the poor themselves in the name of holy poverty?

The solution of the problem may be found in a more perfect exercise of the virtue of detachment. The Church can use its possessions for the relief of poverty. She might fail the poor by refusing to acquire goods or money. Take the example of the largest congregation of religious in the Church. The Sisters of Charity (the ones who used to wear the wide bonnets) live frugally. Their whole organization is directed to serve the poor, the sick and the unfortunate. They have extensive possessions—hospitals, orphanages and convents from which each day the Sisters go out to visit the poor. They also have large institutions in which novices are trained for a life dedicated to charitable work. If all such religious families were to be disbanded the Church could not continue charitable work on the present scale.

With great diffidence I give you a personal example of the dilemma which can arise from efforts to be rid of possessions. When I became Bishop of Leeds I inherited a large house with ample grounds. I soon decided to turn the house into a school for the children of the neighbourhood and went to live as parish priest in a city presbytery. Alas! within a year I realized that this gesture (which gave me great personal satisfaction) was severely hampering my work for souls in the diocese. It was thought that I had lost interest in my major work which was the care of the priests and people of the West Riding of Yorkshire. I subsequently learned that some who needed my help had been reluctant to visit me in the presbytery. At last I realized that duty, like justice, must not only be done but must be seen to be done. The experiment failed. I had to search around the city of Leeds to find another house to which priests and faithful could come without feeling that they were intruding on my parish duties. I mention this personal experience to illustrate the hazard of abandoning possessions without full consideration of pastoral needs. It is good to refuse luxury but wrong to cripple work for souls by dispensing with the material means to accomplish it. Some people thoughtlessly declare that we should build no more churches. It requires little imagination to see that if the Church is a worshipping community it must have some centre of worship. Without a meeting place the community would soon disappear. In a parish of two or three thousand it is unrealistic to say that a priest can serve his flock without a church.

It is, of course, true that our practice of poverty can be puzzling. Church buildings, monasteries and convents are sometimes built extravagantly. An architect cannot be expected to realize the need to plan modestly. Vast sums of money have been spent since the Council on new religious dress and on quite unnecessary national and international conferences. A prioress of a contemplative order once told me that the Rule insists on wooden goblets, which nowadays have to be specially made. In the beginning the nuns used wooden goblets as a sign of poverty. The equivalent of the goblets used by the medieval poor would today be cheap crockery from a local store. An outward show of poverty can defeat the very purpose of poverty.

I suspect you feel that unofficial groups of Christians devoted to poverty are likely to be superior to those acting officially in the name of the Church. We need to be wary of the now rather overworked notion of what is charismatic. The kind of group you describe bound together in the spirit of poverty ('mainly lay people' you say 'with one or two priests among them') are really no improvement on the thousands of groups in the Church (like the society of St Vincent de Paul) whose members undertake works of mercy methodically. Apart from the gratification which is bound to come from honest efforts to relieve distress, there is an immense advantage for the work itself in the discipline imposed by membership of a society or sodality. Those who regard themselves as more effective in a Christian community by remaining outside established societies can actually retard the work of the Church. There are some who carry out the duties of the lay apostolate—I say 'duties' because every Christian is called to be an apostle—merely by fulfilling their domestic or professional duties. It would be wrong for a mother to neglect her family, a craftsman to abstain from the work of his craft or a doctor to leave his patients untended in order to attend meetings of a church organization. For many the apostolate lies in fulfilling their common tasks. Nevertheless those who have time and opportunity should normally serve the community by answering the call to action made by the Church. It is sad when splendid organizations languish for lack of members because able Christians claim to be 'non-joiners'. Catholics, at least, have no right to complain that the Church is idle in carrying out works of mercy if they refuse to volunteer their services.

You say that committees can never be the germ of new life. I agree, if you have in mind that some committees are, as they say, no more than talking shops. People easily come to believe that if they have discussed a problem they have solved it. But there are many groups which talk only in order to act. Two obvious examples are Oxfam and Cafod (Catholic Fund for Overseas Development).

I find it hard to understand what you mean by the frustration of priests and laity because they are refused the opportunity of celebrating the liturgy 'visibly, simply and lovingly'. You say that small groups would provide the leaven for the whole lump of the Church with such a liturgy to give them warmth and dynamic power. It is wise to scrutinise our motives whenever we complain that the Church frustrates our good intentions. It is, of course, more cosy to meet in small groups with kindred souls than to celebrate the liturgy with crowds of people. Priests now commonly celebrate Mass in the homes of their people for the sake of fostering the spirit of community in a neighbourhood. Spontaneously arising groups such as you describe can be excellent but they can also be destructive of true community. If the local Church is dead, if it has ceased to preach the gospel by word and action, it can be saved by a few on fire with zeal for souls—but only if they do not cut themselves off.

It is better, where possible, to revitalize what already exists in the Church than to form private groups. You quote the example of a bishop who failed to encourage a group which was 'enormously rich in brotherly love, practical and effective charity'. I gather that it was primarily a liturgical group and that the bishop's representative reported only deviations from the rubrics and failed to notice the overwhelming atmosphere of joy and love. In my experience joy and love can be either attractive or suspect. The 'junkies' are said to be full of joy and love but they are scarcely beneficial to the community. If we can credit reports from certain parts of the world some liturgical groups are led by clerical anarchists. Fussing over tiny rubrics is reprehensible, but so is an ostentatious contempt for liturgical rules. The Eucharist is our most sacred possession. It was Christ's last testament to his brethren.

The Church would be failing in her duty if she were to allow every Catholic to become his own liturgist. A bishop may become unpopular if, like St Paul, he wants things to be done decently and in order. A rebel priest, on the other hand, may become the idol of his group if he ignores all rubrics, casts aside his priestly vestments and presides at a do-it-yourself Eucharist. Anarchy is popular only among anarchists and has within it the seeds of destruction. A true Catholic regards the Church as a mother with compassion on the millions who live without knowledge of Christ. He would never allow himself the luxury of contracting out of the life of the Church. St Augustine said that if we preserve order

F

it will save us. There is always a great temptation to do things
in our own way rather than in God's. While still an adolescent I thought that I was called to the priesthood. But at my
age the world seemed more attractive. I asked a holy Jesuit
if God ever calls reluctant souls to the priesthood or the
religious life. He told me that most souls are reluctant to
make great sacrifices. We find peace by following God's will
rather than our own inclinations. The public worship of God
must be conducted according to his will.

Now I come to your views about bishops. I must thank
you at once for your compassion. You realize that all too
often bishops are expected to be supermen. It might have
been more accurate to have said that the faithful expect
bishops to be supernatural men, that is, men of outstanding
holiness and spiritual wisdom. Speaking as I must only for
myself, I confess that the faithful are often disappointed.
But, as you wisely point out, the high standard expected of a
bishop is both a compliment and an act of faith. Your description of a bishop as the official life-giver is percipient and
beautiful. I agree that, whether or not he likes it, a bishop
will be judged according to the demands of the symbolic
position he occupies in the Church of God. It would be improper of me to undertake an apologia for the hierarchy. I
think, however, that you are harsh in your judgement—
especially when you say that the people are denied the love
and trust of their bishops. You suggest that bishops are so
concerned with preserving their own authority that they are
reluctant to allow anyone to try anything new. The people,
you allege, feel 'let down' after the Council. From Rome came
the vision of total renewal in the Church. A powerful and
new leadership was to emerge. But, in the event, the bishops
returned with a 'no' on their lips to every initiative. Their
faithful people became disillusioned and embittered.

We are still so close to the Council that it is difficult to see it in perspective. You may not know that the decrees of the Council have been put into practice more promptly in England and Wales than in almost any other country. At a meeting of European bishops held in Holland in the late spring of 1967, our continental colleagues were astonished at the speed of our progress. It may be that we need more help from public relations officers if our priests and people are unaware of all the changes which have already been effected. Apart from reforms in the liturgy (which, if anything, have been too hasty), the Councils of Priests to advise bishops in the running of dioceses were, as far as I know, first set up in Britain. Parish Councils are everywhere being elected. From them will be recruited members for the Diocesan Senates.

Bishops are astonished when complaints are made about their addiction to pomp. You say that the bishop should 'get rid of the clutter in dress and entourage that separates him from the people'. This is something which bothers only a small section of our people. It is voiced mainly in circles which oddly have no objection to academic dress. It is amazing that intelligent people can think that bishops themselves enjoy the fuss and trappings or regard them as important in themselves. Those who worry about such inessentials make themselves mildly absurd. One tiny group in England solemnly campaigns to remove from priests the title 'Father' in favour of 'Brother' or 'Mister'. I assure you I have not invented this group. There do actually exist people so out of touch with Catholic feeling as to wish to rob the priest of the beautiful title he shares with the Holy Father.

Bishops are usually indifferent about the robes they wear and are naturally happiest when out of uniform. Like soldiers, barristers or bus conductors, they dress according to their rank mainly for the convenience of the public they serve. When not on duty, bishops dress in black. When they visit a parish they wear purple and use the mitre and crozier. Anyone who seeks to abolish these symbols on the grounds that the faithful are put off by them can have little knowledge of the faithful. Wise people do not allow uniforms to become an obsession. Judges, mayors and others in positions of authority are expected to wear some badge of office. Priests masquerading as laymen or bishops refusing to wear their robes make themselves popular with rebels but merely confuse and sadden the rest of the people of God. Bishops wear distinctive dress but if they could better serve God and their people in sackcloth they would gladly wear it.

You appeal for a more democratic government of the Church. In some ways, as I shall mention, democracy has been decreed by the Vatican Council and in large measure has already been put into practice. But the Council did not canonize democracy, because the Church was not founded by Christ as a specifically democratic institution. When as part of their apostolate the laity work with the priest or the priests with their bishop, ultimate responsibility must remain with the parish priest or diocesan bishop. There are no words of Christ in the gospel instructing the Church to be ruled by majority decisions. That is why the Council was careful to point out that the Parish Council is an instrument to advise the parish priest, the Council of Clergy and Diocesan Senate to advise the bishop, and the Synod of Bishops to advise the Pope. Never forget that priests and bishops are usually men whose whole thought and training have been directed towards pastoral work. An experienced pastor of souls is therefore more likely than a bank clerk or teacher of chemistry to know what is best for souls. Of course the parishioners and diocesans should be encouraged to give their opinion and lend their skills. But those whom God has called to the priesthood are not at liberty to shirk ultimate responsibility:

'The Holy Ghost hath placed you bishops to rule the Church of God' (Acts xx, 28).

You think that difficulties might be resolved if bishops were elected and if elected representatives were appointed to help them. The elected representatives are already a reality. The Council of Clergy in each diocese is composed mainly of priests elected by their colleagues. The composition of Parish Councils is necessarily still experimental. This is mainly because it is easier to advocate than to organize elections. The chief difficulty in the Catholic community is to induce the laity to accept responsibility. It will take more than a generation to persuade most ordinary Catholic laymen not to leave pastoral affairs to the priest. There is the further difficulty that there are many of the better educated— not excluding those educated on State grants and scholarships—who hold themselves aloof from humble parish activities. They prefer to join select groups which offer criticism rather than service. In the end the priest in most parishes secures the election of a Parish Council only by repeated pleading with suitable candidates to take an active interest in what God through the Council is saying to the churches. If the most talented stand aside it will be impossible to show the world that the Church really meant what she said in the famous Decree on the Church in the Modern World. You rightly urge that the laity must feel involved. But if the official means of involvement are spurned, the objectives of the Council will never be attained.

There is no doubt that the Church is in earnest about involving the laity in all that affects the good of souls. But it does not follow that bishops should abstain from making decisions except in public debate. It is true that we have not yet sufficiently learned that much of the secrecy imposed by authority is self-defeating. It still too often happens that documents are issued under a needless seal of secrecy. A recent example is the agenda for the first meeting of the Synod of Bishops. Apart from the fact that documents issued in thousands are bound at some time to become public, it is hard to see why the subjects to be discussed could not have been made known from the beginning to the clergy and faithful. As well as being teachers and guardians the bishops are also witnesses to the faith of their flocks. It takes time to alter the habits of centuries, but increasingly the bishops make known and seek advice on all matters affecting their people. Thus Friday abstinence was subjected to a canvass of opinion before formally coming to the hierarchy of England and Wales for decision.

The question of the election of bishops which you raise is deceptively simple. When the Church was small and made up of clearly separate communities it was natural and easy for leaders to be chosen by popular acclaim. It would be difficult to discover any really practical method of electing bishops today. I take it that the right of suffrage would have to be granted to all the clergy and faithful of a diocese. It would be considered unprogressive and, indeed, intolerable in these democratic days to have a restricted suffrage. It is likely, therefore, since most people know only the priests who minister to them, that the most popular priests in the biggest parishes would receive the largest number of votes. This might, of course, result in the election of the most suitable candidates but we must recognize certain disadvantages in such a system.

As a bishop who has been appointed to three Sees (none of which is the diocese for which I was ordained) it would be disingenuous if I were to maintain that a priest from elsewhere is always best fitted to rule a diocese. I am bound to say, however, that I doubt the wisdom of confining the choice to the priests of the diocese. As a member of the Consistorial Congregation (which makes the final recommenda-

tion of candidates to the Holy Father) I know that it is sometimes most desirable to give a diocese a priest from outside
or to transfer an existing bishop. I would be sorry if a system
were introduced which made it virtually impossible to seek
bishops from among the members of religious congregations.
Experience has proved that a religious, although comparatively unknown to the faithful, may bring great gifts to a diocese and incidentally enrich the national hierarchy. I suspect
that those who advocate the election of bishops either have
not sufficiently weighed the consequences or have in mind a
restricted suffrage. What would be an acceptable basis of
entitlement to vote—income? I.Q.? Mass attendance? Membership of Catholic societies? It must be universal suffrage or
nothing.

You may not know how very wide an investigation is carried out by the Holy See before episcopal appointments are
made. That is one reason for the long delays before a vacant
See is filled. Confidential opinions—and this is an example of
secrecy which is not only desirable but essential—are sought
from bishops, clergy and laity. Although mistakes occur, the
process of choosing bishops is prudent and just. The names
of three candidates (*terna*) are submitted to the Consistorial
Congregation with full details of the character and qualifications of each candidate. The Consistorial is no rubber stamp.
I have seen the order of candidates reversed and also the
whole *terna* rejected. When a vacancy arises and the *terna* is
being prepared, clergy and faithful are at liberty to write to
the Papal Nuncio or Apostolic Delegate making known their
views. No information is withheld when the reports are prepared for the Consistorial Congregation. It is hard to believe
that local elections would be more satisfactory. A fair election on a universal suffrage could scarcely be conducted without some sort of canvassing on behalf of possible candidates.
At the top of the poll an apparently ideal candidate could

emerge whom the Holy See from confidential information might know to be quite unsuitable. It would be possible to extend the range of the official enquiries, but confidential information cannot prudently be too widely sought. It was not out of caprice that the Church discontinued the practice of electing bishops.

You end by referring to criticism within the Church and to the crisis of authority. In Britain the crisis is less evident than in certain other countries, while in places where the Church suffers persecution bishops, priests and faithful are more united than ever before. This I have learned from bishops behind the so-called Iron Curtain. Despite the grumbles of clergy and faithful about each other and about their bishops, despite the publicity sought by priests in revolt, the Church in this country remains relatively peaceful. But, of course, a hundred families united in love do not attract even a small paragraph in the newspapers. Lawbreakers and wreckers of family life, on the other hand, capture the headlines. It would nevertheless be foolish to discount the importance of unrecorded harmony in the hundred families. Criticism is good provided it is honest, constructive and charitable. We have spoken freely without any desire to score or to wound. That is why I think it was worth while to write this book. I thank you for agreeing to collaborate with me in a task whose object was to add dignity and meaning to that worn out word 'dialogue'.

Cardinal Heenan

Early in June 1967 I set aside a few days in which to complete my part of this book. On the very first day a severe headache made it difficult for me to concentrate. By the weekend my bed was surrounded by puzzled doctors. Shortly before midnight on the Sunday I was put in an ambulance and taken to St Thomas's Hospital in London. The diagnosis was encephalitis which, despite modern drugs, is still a killing disease. I was anointed and received Holy Viaticum. By Wednesday, although still weak, I was in no immediate danger. How much was due to cortisone and how much to the prayers generously offered by thousands of friends throughout the world is God's secret.

Being (as I thought) close to death enabled me to see truth with a new clarity. I had always imagined that the approach of death would be disturbing. Apparent danger of death need not, of course, create the same sensations as the approach of death itself. Nevertheless, since I did not know whether I was to recover or die, the experience was unique and valuable. I was surprised that I felt no fear and that praying did not become difficult. I have assisted at the death of many devout Catholics and usually they found it hard to pray. Some, indeed, had to battle with temptations against the faith—but these were exceptionally holy people. Disinclination to pray is mainly caused by physical weakness induced by long suffering. I came to my crisis comparatively fresh. I was still able to grasp and gain strength and comfort from my crucifix and rosary. I enjoyed great peace of mind.

It is said that the whole of his life comes in swift review before the eyes of a drowning man. This is probably a myth and, since nobody has returned from an ocean grave, we cannot tell. Mercifully my whole life did not flash back—otherwise I would not have enjoyed such peace of mind. Some events, however, did return quite vividly. These mainly concerned the Church—which is not surprising since only a few days earlier all my thoughts had been on this book. I also saw in a detached way scenes of my life as a boy, priest and bishop. While the virus remained in control the kaleidoscope had no more consistency than a nightmare. But once the crisis was over I experienced a kind of waking dream—very different from the hallucinations of the first fevered hours—which had some sort of logical sequence. The first persistent thoughts concerned the few Catholics who ceaselessly attack all in authority in the Church of God.

For the first time I saw them as people in need of compassion. Hitherto I had found it hard to excuse those who had declared war on bishops, pastoral clergy, religious superiors and on all unexciting laymen who are content to say their prayers and support the apostolate in their parishes. Such people were scorned as ignorant of the real meaning of Christianity. A sadistic mood seemed to have taken possession of a small set. For them the old faith had become something of a joke, the Church as our mother a figure of fun. Within the Church the 'structures'—a favourite word—were all wrong. Praise was reserved for those daring sons of the Church who had become apostates. The only enlightened attitude towards the Church was one of constant abuse.

During these first days in hospital I was unable to read. I therefore had leisure to look at the problem in a detached sort of way. Dr Johnson remarked that when a man knows he is to be hanged in a fortnight it concentrates his mind wonderfully. The approach of death helps disinterested thinking. I shall try in all honesty to give without embellishment the thoughts which came unbidden as I lay in hospital. I found myself thinking first of these embittered Catholics who during the last two or three years have so restlessly denounced all bishops—not excluding the Bishop of Rome. I thought of them without anger or distaste. I sought excuses for them. I wondered how in England where we had always enjoyed remarkable charity within the Church such passionate hostility could ever have arisen. This, after all, was not just the intemperance often associated with religious controversy. Nor would there be anything remarkable in self-assertiveness among those for whom theology is still a novelty. The disturbing feature is that the unqualified set themselves up as authorities. Everyone suddenly feels free to pontificate —if I may use the word—on every dogmatic, moral and pastoral problem. A Protestant mentality has evolved. A Catholic is told to be guided only by his own private interpretation of doctrine. Each man is the teaching Church. The magisterium is out-of-date and irrelevant.

A pleasant background to these hospital thoughts was provided by a bedside radio. Sickness had provided me with an opportunity of listening to the classical music broadcast all through the day by the B.B.C. Never since ordination had I enjoyed so much leisure. In good conscience I need do nothing but listen to these brilliantly devised programmes. One composer is chosen for a whole week during which a thoroughly representative selection of his work is heard, together with comments from experts. As I listened to their commentaries, I could not help comparing these musicologists with some contemporary exponents of theology. The Church rejoices at the growing interest of the public in theology but when amateurs set themselves up as experts they become a liability to any institution whether religious or secular.

Theology has not been enriched by the work of modern dilettantes. Nobody thinks of writing about music, I reflected as I listened to the radio, with a comparable lack of qualification. After attending half a dozen promenade concerts to hear selections from Benjamin Britten, Vaughan Williams and Elgar, nobody would feel qualified to write a book on musical appreciation. Before presuming to teach, a wise man would study musical theory, learn all about harmony and, above all, soak himself in the works of such masters as Bach, Mozart, Beethoven, Handel and Wagner. Many now writing on theology have no acquaintance with classical theology or the works of the Fathers who are the masters of theology. I wondered how many writers of paperbacks have ever opened Migne's Latin or Greek Patrology. Purely speculative theology requires no patristic scholarship. That is why lecturers who would not think of publishing works on their own disciplines can pose as religious pundits. Since the Council there has been a rash of books of new theology. Few of the authors are serious theologians. A Congar or a Rahner has not invented a new theology. They have enriched and freshened the old. It is only the lesser men who produce extravagant theories and dare to call them, in the literal sense, gospel truth. Translations of the writings of second-rate continental theologians have persuaded theological illiterates in the English-speaking world that they can become prophets without the hard grind of a theological training. Such speculators (and, of course, their eager publishers) are responsible for much of the current confusion among educated Catholics. It is fashionable to blame the professionals but, in fact, the professional theologians (most of whose names are unknown outside seminaries and universities) are the Church's salvation.

These reflexions arose from consideration of the lack of charity, amounting on occasion to hatred, of a few Catholics towards the hierarchy and pastoral clergy. They advocate the abolition of almost all the means by which the Church has hitherto built up the spiritual life of her children. Dioceses and parishes are said, in their jargon, to have lost 'credibility'. Members of religious orders have so far escaped the lash but inevitably they, too, will be excoriated for concentrating on educating sons of the well-to-do. Wherever Catholics gather is labelled a ghetto. The hierarchy is reactionary (or corrupt) for not tearing down all existing Catholic institutions. This attitude makes mockery of the teaching of Pope John, yet those who claim to have his spirit delight in sins against charity which in rather undergraduate fashion they call 'bishop bashing'. Unfortunately they are encouraged by 'advanced' clerics who being without a pastoral charge have no contact with normal Catholic life. Members of this resentful group never speak anything good of the Church. Their articles and letters are welcomed by anti-Catholic editors. Even religious journals seem blind to offences against charity. An example has come to hand as I write. It is from an article, 'Authority in the Church' in *New Blackfriars*. The writer, a member of *The Tablet* staff, attacking the hierarchy, alleges that 'some of our bishops still like to be addressed and treated with the deference due to a mediaeval robber-baron'. It is not so much the libel as the utter lack of charity (as well as pietas and politeness) which is disheartening. Yet the article —a lecture on how those with authority in the Church should use it—ends by making a plea for charity so that 'how these Christians love one another will no longer be a cynical jibe'. Originally, of course, this was not a jibe but an expression of the pagans' admiration for the mutual love among Christians. A biblical test of what is charitable is given by St Paul: 'Charity is patient and kind ... never boastful or conceited, never rude' (1 Cor. xiii, 13).

Being more or less in the shadow of death I was anxious to see what in my own life had been lacking. I thought of my sixteen years as a bishop and of some of the mistakes I have made. I realized, of course, that of my worst mistakes I am probably unaware. The great handicap of new bishops is to have received no specialized training. It is hard to see how this can be remedied. In the army 'officer material', as it is called, is transferred from the ranks to units for special tuition. It would be embarrassing, to say the least, if likely young priests were thus segregated. One method of training might be to send the bishop-designate to be trained by an experienced bishop. But even this would not really help. A new bishop is always given advice and help by his colleagues but the actual conduct of his own diocese he must learn for himself. Despite years of seminary life a priest learns more during his first three months in a parish than from the years of theoretical training. Bishops also learn mainly from experience. This means, in effect, that they learn from their mistakes. I made many mistakes in the exercise of authority when first I was sent to Leeds. I had been superior of the Catholic Missionary Society with nine or ten priest members. When I became a bishop I was to discover the vast difference between leading a small team of chosen volunteers and a diocese of four hundred clergy both diocesan and regular.

Before concentrating on my life as a bishop in Leeds, Liverpool and Westminster my mind went back to the early years when I was mercifully unaware that one day I must bear the awesome burden of prelacy. My earliest memories

were revived. The dying not uncommonly imagine themselves back among the scenes of their childhood. My mind
was not so much wandering as conducting a kind of spiritual
self-survey. I was looking at the religious events which had
helped to form my outlook on the priesthood. I must record
that although it may sound unlikely my First Communion
Day came vividly to mind. Whether or not it was the happiest
day of Napoleon's life it was certainly the happiest of mine
—except for the day when first I celebrated Holy Mass. I
saw the picture of Father Palmer, the parish priest, proud
and happy as he spoke to us children before Mass began. It
was the ninth of February in 1913, the year before the
Great War.

The church was SS Peter and Paul's, Ilford, Essex. In
those days Ilford was a country town. The parish was a family
in which most people knew each other and all were known to
the parish priest. I had been given a small prayer book with a
white cover on which was a highly coloured picture of the
Sacred Heart. It was the gift of Mrs Lynch, a family friend,
who many years later was to have three Jesuit sons and a
daughter a Servite nun. I remembered standing outside the
church with my parents after Mass, feeling very holy and
important. We children were soon called into the school hall
adjoining the church but, much as I was looking forward to
cake and custard for breakfast, I was reluctant to leave my
family and friends. In the evening we had a procession of the
Blessed Sacrament for which we First Communicants wore
red sashes to show how very special we were. I hope that no
mistaken ecumenism will ever call for the abolition of First
Communion Day in favour of Confirmation Day (or of a
Solemn Communion on the French model) when children
'are old enough to understand what they are doing'. However
long we live we can never fully understand the holy Eucharist
nor ever be more worthy to receive the Body of Christ than in

the days of our innocence. First Communion Day, as I was to discover as parish priest, can be the most fruitful pastoral occasion in the life of a family and a parish.

I thought next of Ushaw, the seminary I entered at the age of seventeen after leaving the Jesuit school at Stamford Hill. One of the chief lessons I learned at Ushaw was the meaning of an adult devotion to our Lady. In an undemonstrative way the whole atmosphere seemed to foster awareness of Mary, Queen of Apostles. From the example of the priests on the staff—especially old Mgr Browne the President—I also learned the value of personal prayer. I had, of course, been taught to pray, as the saying goes, at my mother's knee. I still have my Garden of the Soul with the pages of the Thirty Days' Prayer blackened by my grubby fingers. I had recited this daily from an early age for the grace one day to become a holy priest. I had never heard of meditation until I went to the seminary. Meditation, as such, meant little—but the quiet prayer before Mass became a source of great strength. Hitherto I had almost always prayed with book in hand. Experience was to show me that any book—even the bible or the breviary—can become intrusive and therefore an obstacle to union with God.

When two years later I was sent to the English College in Rome, I found once more that great stress was laid on personal prayer. Here again the teaching came mainly from the example of an old rector. Mgr Hinsley was not, in fact, very old but he was bald. To a boy of nineteen a bald man in his fifties looks very old indeed. No students of the Hinsley regime could ever forget the importance of morning prayer. The first fruits of the day, the rector insisted, must be offered to Almighty God. Almost any breach of the rules was regarded as minor by comparison with missing meditation. A student too slothful to rise in time to pray was unlikely, in the rector's view, to become a fervent priest. Monsignor

Hinsley was very far from under-estimating the importance of the intellectual formation of his students. He took a sometimes uncomfortably keen interest in our progress at the university. Second-rate performance was rebuked in harsh fashion and a man suspected of slackness was in great danger of being sent home. Nevertheless it was impossible for the future priest to doubt that his spiritual formation was the rector's first concern.

Like all educational institutes the Gregorian University has raised its standards since the years just after the first world war. In seven years it was then possible to acquire a doctorate in both philosophy and theology. The system of lectures had not changed substantially since the seventeenth century. On most days we had to endure three or four lectures of an hour's duration. Apart from a certain facility in speaking Latin, most of us felt that we gained too little from the lectures. We regarded the plurality of lectures as a relic of the days before printing was widespread. Most of our solid work was done at home during the ample hours of private study. To be in Rome for so long was in itself a liberal education. All roads, it is said, lead to Rome and many distinguished visitors were persuaded to give talks at the English College.

During the seven years most students returned only once to England. The disadvantage of this segregation from home was compensated by frequent opportunities of travel. There are few better ways of fostering initiative than touring with small resources and the students went on walking tours whenever possible. Most of the long summer vacation (in those days the university did not open until the end of October) was spent at Palazzola, a delightful villa overlooking Lake Albano. The discipline at the villa was relaxed but a great deal of our time was devoted to serious reading. There were sermon groups, Dante clubs and musical appreciation societies. Many students acquired the rudiments of new languages. Altogether it was a pleasant and rewarding interlude in the severe scholastic routine of Rome.

For some cause hard to diagnose the only episode in my Roman life which came at all graphically to mind was the occasion when I took the oral (viva) examination for the Ph.D. I saw myself sitting at a green baize-covered table facing the four Jesuit examiners: Munzi (Italian), Lehman (German), Boyer (French) and Hoenen (Dutch). A candidate for the doctorate had before him a list of a hundred propositions (theses). Each professor in turn chose a proposition which the student was expected to establish and defend against all arguments. When I sat down I was asked to defend the shortest thesis in the list: *Deus habet influxum immediatum in omni actione humana* (No human action takes place without God's direct collaboration). This is Thomistic doctrine but some philosophers, including Suarez, disagree with the word 'direct'. The point at issue may be of small interest or importance today but it was of great moment to me on that hot June morning in 1927. I declined the thesis on the grounds that it was indefensible. I rose to go away unexamined but the professors bade me stay while they conferred. After a few moments the presiding examiner said: 'We would not ask a young man to defend a thesis against his own convictions. We therefore want you to take a thesis of your own choice.' As I have said, I cannot tell why this incident came back to me in hospital. It is possible that unconsciously I was reflecting that the professors in Rome were not so unfeeling as everyone in authority in Rome is alleged to be. The iniquity of Roman officials has become an article of faith for the critics of the Church.

I wondered in later years why I had not been sent away to learn humility. I was only twenty-two and if at that age I thought I knew better than Aquinas I might think that I knew better than the Church in my more mature years. In the event the tolerant examiners were probably more amused than alarmed. This recollection took me back, for some reason, to my adolescence. Fifty years ago there was far less social contact between Catholics and non-Catholics than there is today. A Catholic child wanting to bring home a new friend would almost certainly be asked about his religion. Catholics were usually on close terms with non-Catholics only if they were relatives. It happened that my relatives living in England were Protestants (my grandmother was a convert). Among them was a married cousin who had no children and treated me almost as a son. He was a civil servant and during my most formative years was in charge of the Science Museum in South Kensington. He set out to enlarge my outlook and, as he used to say, to remove the blinkers imposed by my Church. He was giving me Bertrand Russell to read when I was only sixteen. Although his influence was in some ways disturbing, it proved of considerable value to me in later years. He tried to teach me never to accept what seemed intellectually unsatisfactory.

Next I was recalling my years as curate and parish priest. (I realize that this record has no historical sequence. I have refrained from touching it up because it is important to give my thoughts just as they came to me in hospital.) After ordination I spent a further year in Rome to take a doctorate in theology. I was then appointed assistant priest in the parish of Barking. In all I was to spend more than sixteen years in the East End of London. They were fruitful and happy years. Since the Council some have begun to ask what is the function of a priest. A little pastoral experience will supply the answer. The priest is not just a relieving officer, doctor or lawyer, although his ministry will be largely in the service of the poor, sick and afflicted. It is the sublime privilege of the

Catholic priest to be father and friend to young and old. To the local non-Catholic public he is the Catholic Church. To the fervent Catholic he is another Christ. 'Let a man so account of us as of the ministers of Christ and the dispensers of the mysteries of God' (I Cor. iv, 1). Even lapsed Catholics recognize the priest as a man of God. The faithful trust and cherish him so long as he shows himself to be a man of God. The priest whose preaching is restricted to the pulpit, who fails to visit his people to talk and pray with them and bring God's message, will not win the confidence and love of his people. Only such a priest need be uncertain about his function and status. He may seek consolation by trying to forget his priesthood. But the priest who plays the layman is even more pitiable than the layman who resents the position of the priest.

The precious title of father which the faithful accord their priests symbolizes the warmth of pastoral relationship within the Catholic Church. Celibacy of the clergy partly explains why the priest is so readily accepted as a member of every family. He belongs entirely to his people. There is no wife or child to whom he has prior obligations. Married clergy in other denominations may often be worthier and more industrious but the position of the Catholic priest in the west is unique. Unless he neglects his people they will give him their love in a measure which astounds those outside the Church. During my years in Barking and Manor Park I had abundant proof of the devotion of Catholics towards their priests. When I began parochial work in 1931 there was still considerable unemployment. Even today in the welfare state there can be pitiful distress among old people living alone and in the families of widows. There is still need for compassionate assistance, but a quarter of a century ago deprivation was widespread.

Recalling conditions in London in the thirties I remembered how favourable they were to the spread of communism. Soviet Russia, as yet little visited, was plausibly presented as the paradise of the workers. Communist propaganda disguised the vicious nature of Stalin's Russia. I felt that it would be useful to visit the U.S.S.R. in order to speak about Soviet communism with some authority. After two unsuccessful attempts to secure a visa I sailed in a Soviet boat from London to Leningrad in October 1936. For the purposes of my Russian tour I described myself as a psychologist and one of my first appointments was with Professor Pavlov who demonstrated his famous dogs with their conditioned reflexes. By chance I was in the Soviet Union at the height of Stalin's great purge—Kamenev, Zinoviev, Radek and many of the old Bolshevik guard were all 'liquidated' about that time. This doubtless helped me to avoid detection. The Russians were watching each other with such suspicion that a foreigner was less closely observed. On my return I had enough first-hand information to give my people a fuller picture of the Soviet paradise.

It was not until after ordination that I came across any large number of Catholics who had ceased to practise their religion. When I was very young comparatively few failed to attend Mass. Almost all the school children were regular in their spiritual duties. The parish priest was resolute in his opposition to a Mass register and a children's Mass. The public spirit of school and parish made it unlikely that many would fall away. That, of course, was Ilford before the first world war. Barking before the second world war presented a far different picture. The proportion of lapsed was distressingly high although the number of practising and enthusiastic Catholics was still higher. Attendance at evening services and confraternity meetings was excellent. There were two schools and a hospital in the parish and my fellow curate and I (the parish priest was more or less an invalid) had little leisure. After the first few months, however, I was able to fashion a rule of life in which reading and, later, writing had a place. In 1935 I began writing my first book. It was a pastoral study of the sacrament of Penance entitled *Priest and Penitent*. It was published in 1937 by Sheed and Ward. This firm was then in its golden period. Chesterton, Belloc, Dawson, Hughes, Hollis and almost all Catholic writers of the day were anxious to support the enterprise of Frank Sheed and Maisie Ward, who were themselves writers of distinction. Because of these authors with guaranteed sales the publishers were able to encourage young and unknown Catholic writers. That is how my book came to be accepted. In later years the same firm was to publish more of my books.

My native parish in Essex was in the diocese of Westminster, but during the first world war it became part of the newly created diocese of Brentwood. When I was a young priest the number of clergy in Brentwood was small. This had the considerable advantage that priests were given parishes in their early thirties instead of having to await middle age. Thus at the age of thirty-two I was made parish priest of Manor Park. The people gave me a typically Catholic welcome as I began a term of office which was to last over ten years. As I lay in hospital continuing my silent soliloquy—if that is not a contradiction in terms—I came back to the war years in Manor Park. I had gone there with a sense of relief, because at that time Cardinal Hinsley was pressing me to become his secretary. I was willing to meet his wishes but my heart was in parish work. I was therefore immensely relieved when the Bishop of Brentwood refused to release me. As a student I had thought that every priest is bound to his own diocese for life. It did not require the Second Vatican Council to teach me that a priest must be ready to go anywhere. I had been ordained only three years when the Holy See asked me to become secretary to the newly appointed Apostolic Delegate in Africa. Though lacking all enthusiasm for the diplomatic service I had naturally agreed to go. Happily the nomination of the Apostolic Delegate himself was cancelled soon afterwards and my own posting therefore lapsed.

Life in the East End of London after 1939 was sometimes unpleasant—especially during the frequent bombing of the docks—yet those wartime years were among the happiest of my life. We all know in theory that there is nothing more beautiful than true brotherhood, but to see it in practice is like a relevation. All through the war the people in the borough of East Ham (of which Manor Park was part) were exemplary in their mutual charity. By the end of the war both my churches had been severely hit, the school was bombed and not a single house in the town remained undamaged. Widespread suffering drew people together in a remarkable way. It was a community not of misery but of joy. Each night during the many months of the blitz some homes were destroyed. It was then that the charity of neighbours showed itself. The homeless were cherished, clothed and sheltered. There was, at the same time, an impressive unity among the people of every type and persuasion. I came to know them all in the first-aid posts and shelters. 'Welcome, Father' they would say in greeting and 'God bless you, Father' when I left. These people were mostly nominal Protestants and un-orthodox Jews but the hardships of war had made them feel that they all belonged to one family. They took their cue from their Catholic neighbours in their attitude towards the priests. Hence the affection and respect—and the comfort they derived from our presence in moments of peril. In my heart I regarded them all as members of my flock. It is always consoling to have love returned and that is why I can say sincerely that these were really happy years despite the constant threat from enemy action.

There were three clerics affectionately known as the three musketeers. The Rev. Stanley Pink (now Archdeacon of Hampstead) was the Anglican Rector. The Rev. Alfred Binks (who died some ten years after the war) was the Minister of the Methodist Central Hall. I was the third of the trio. Ecumenism had scarcely been heard of at that time, but we three practised it without constraint or embarrassment. When their hall was commandeered by the army we offered the Anglican youth the use of ours. The rector invited our children to use the cellars of his rectory as an air-raid shelter. The local education authorities were anxious that all school children should leave London for evacuation centres and feared lest the provision of shelters might encourage them to remain. The call of home proved in the event far stronger than the fear of bombs. The evacuation schemes failed long before the end of the war. Although officially closed, our school was kept open and assorted volunteers joined my staff. The rector's air-raid shelter was most acceptable.

At the most critical period of the war, when invasion seemed imminent, the King appointed one Sunday as a national day of prayer. Doubtless impending danger as much as spiritual motives moved citizens to a quite remarkable attendance at church and chapel. Subsequent national days of prayer were comparative failures. Even after victory there were few Samaritans found to return thanks. In fact the proportion was evangelical—about one in ten. On the first great day of prayer we three clergy in Manor Park held an impressive United Service in the local recreation grounds. The men and women of the A.R.P. (Air Raid Precautions), auxiliary firemen and police, nurses and doctors marched to the grounds in a great procession accompanied by local bands. We selected hymns common to the Hymns Ancient and Modern, the Methodist Hymn Book and the Westminster Hymnal. Prayers were recited by the rector, the Rev A.

Binks read the bible and I preached the sermon. That all happened over a quarter of a century ago. It is therefore strange to hear it said now that before the Council there was nothing but hostility between Catholics and other Christians. It is time for the history of Christian Unity to be de-mythologized.

There also came to mind another early experiment in ecumenism. After the 1944 Education Act (which introduced the agreed syllabus of religious instruction in State schools), an inter-denominational committee was set up by the non-Catholic clergy. In the borough of East Ham there were several Catholic schools but no other church schools. For this reason, although I was co-opted member of the East Ham Education Committee, no other religious body was represented. There was consequently nobody but myself to speak for the clergy who were compiling an agreed syllabus of religious teaching for local use. The clergy therefore invited me to attend their discussions as an observer—to use the modern description—and I was able to put forward their views at meetings of the education committee. Thus even without the guidance of post-conciliar experiments, the spirit of ecumenism was very evident in that part of London. Then, as now, absence of bigotry greatly served the Christian cause.

An uncovenanted bonus arising from wartime conditions in the parish was increased time for reading and writing. In the East End of London during much of the war life revolved round the air raids. First came the blitz, which for many months was a nightly visitation. There were also occasional daylight raids, but most enemy activity took place during the hours of darkness. Once the bombs began to fall a priest was busy at the scene of the 'incidents' and thereafter at first-aid posts and hospitals. As the war progressed London was attacked by pilotless planes loaded with explosives (popularly called doodlebugs) and rockets (which coming at a speed faster than sound were heard only on impact). Inevitably a great deal of time was spent in the presbytery waiting for air raid warnings. I was thus able in good conscience to spend many more hours at my desk than would have been possible in normal conditions. I published two small books of broadcasts, a memoir of Cardinal Hinsley and a volume on Christian doctrine called *Letters from Rush Green* (the American title was *The Faith makes Sense*). So when peace returned, something had been salvaged from the wreckage of war.

All these recollections of the war years came back to me in hospital. I next recalled the sad day soon after the war when Cardinal Griffin telephoned from a meeting of the hierarchy. The Catholic Missionary Society had virtually ceased to exist. All its priests had been recalled to serve either in the parishes or the armed forces. Missions had been suspended because of the black-out and the other hazards of evening gatherings. The headquarters of the C.M.S. having been requisitioned, the future of the society was uncertain. The former superior, the late Fr Owen Dudley, was no longer young and there was much talk of not reviving the society at all. The Apostolic Delegate, however, urged the bishops to make some attempt to keep it in being. Hence the call from the Cardinal. I remembered the brief conversation almost exactly:

> *Cardinal:* The bishops want you to be superior of the Catholic Missionary Society.
>
> *Me:* I've never had anything to do with the C.M.S. so how could I become Superior?
>
> *Cardinal:* You would have to start from scratch and build up a new team. You have twenty-four hours in which to make up your mind.
>
> *Me:* What is the idea of the twenty-four hours?

Cardinal: Some of the bishops thought you might hate
to leave Manor Park and so we decided to give you time
to think.

Me: I wonder what led anyone to imagine that in twenty-
four hours I would feel more like leaving the parish? I
don't need time to decide. If the hierarchy wants me to
go, that is enough.

It may surprise those who are critical of the clergy to
learn that this attitude was and remains typical of diocesan
priests dealing with their bishops. Almost any priest does
what he is asked without delay. This, incidentally, is another
social situation which needs demythologizing. Bishops and
clergy are, in fact, normally united in loyal service to their
people. The hard, unfeeling, institutionalized relationships
exist largely in the imagination of the pastorally in-
experienced.

Little of what happened during the following three years
in the Catholic Missionary Society came to my mind. Preaching and visiting families throughout the country naturally
give missionary priests a knowledge of the Catholic Church
in England which could not be supplied by any sociological
survey. Confined to hospital it is perhaps not remarkable that
I thought only of the missions we used to preach in prisons.
In 1949 in preparation for the centenary celebrations of the
restoration of the hierarchy (1850) a mission was preached
in every parish in the country. In addition to the preaching
orders large numbers of other priests and religious volun-
teered to give missions. So that all sections of the Church
might have an opportunity of taking part in the national
mission a petition was sent to the Home Secretary, the enlightened Mr Chuter Ede, asking leave to arrange a mission
in all prisons and borstals. Leave was granted, to the great
spiritual gain of both prisoners and missioners. The prisoners

were shown that the Church as a mother would not exclude from the family renewal those who had been convicted of crime.

Then came some memories of my sixteen years as a bishop. At this time, as I have said, I was preoccupied with the attacks on bishops which have been given such publicity in recent times. As I examined my conscience, my mistakes and failures came vividly to mind. Since these, apart from public utterances, concerned my dealings with priests and people under my care, I forbear to give details. Sufficient to say that being clothed in purple does not make a man less subject to temptation. His temperament, prejudices and weaknesses remain obstacles to the good he wishes to achieve. Soon after becoming a bishop I had realized that high office with its increased responsibilities demands much self-discipline. As the range of work for souls increases there is also a correspondingly greater need for prayer. The fatherhood of a bishop is more than a theological phrase. The well-being of his priests and people is constantly in his thoughts and prayers. It is not difficult to depute certain pastoral tasks to willing priests and laity, but the ultimate responsibility cannot be shed. What St Paul describes as 'the care of all the churches' is in due measure the lot of every bishop. Most of what he does is, in the strictest sense of the word, pastoral. Going round the parishes to encourage his clergy and people, visiting the sick and aged, offering counsel and consolation to the many who come to him with their problems are not activities which he can carry out by proxy. Etymologically the bishop is an overseer but his ministry would be impoverished if he merely supervised the pastoral work of others.

One day in a bishop's life is much like another. Little that is noteworthy of my ministry in Leeds, Liverpool and Westminster came back to me. The routine in each diocese was much the same. I felt that there was little need to repent for being too remote from priests and people. Bishops are not in the least like staff officers at a safe distance from the battle. Three occasions I remembered being out of touch when I was abroad engaged on work of an unusual kind. These came back to me in hospital but did not trouble my conscience.

In 1953 when Bishop of Leeds I was invited by the Australian hierarchy to preach at the National Eucharistic Congress in Sydney. I felt that such a journey would be excessively long for the sake of delivering a few sermons and lectures. I therefore wrote to the War Office offering to make a visitation, on my way to Australia, of the British and Commonwealth troops fighting in Malaya and Korea. This tour took about two months and was, I think, of spiritual value not only to the officers and men of the three services but to the chaplains, who were much encouraged by a visit from one of their own bishops. The chief beneficiary was myself. No amount of literature about war and service life can supply the knowledge which comes from personal experience.

My second long absence was from the diocese of Liverpool to which I had been transferred in 1957. Soon afterwards the immigration of West Indians to the United Kingdom (they always refer to England as the U.K.) had become so great as to produce social problems. Our hierarchy therefore decided to send me to the Caribbean. With the co-operation of local governors I was able to give broadcast talks to prepare intending emigrants for the conditions they were likely to meet in this country. At that time these poor people often arrived dressed in cotton without the means of buying warm clothes for the winter. I was also able to set up some modest organizations in Jamaica, British Guiana (as it was then called) and Trinidad (where the Legion of Mary was strong) to arrange for the strangers to be met at the ports. Owing to the vast numbers involved all too little was achieved. My journey came to mind nevertheless as an example of the hierarchy's compassion for those in need. (The bishops many years before had set up, under the far from nominal direction of the Bishop of Nottingham, an efficient organization to meet the spiritual and temporal needs of the thousands of refugees from European countries.)

The most prolonged absences were during the Council. These did not come back to me in hospital but I did recall the meetings before the Council began. I was a member of the Secretariat for Christian Unity. We were not at first a large number and therefore came to know each other well. Despite differences of race and culture we soon became a well-knit group. In these early days the representation from the English-speaking world was remarkably small. There was no bishop from U.S.A., Canada, Australia, New Zealand or India. From Africa there was only an English-speaking Dutch Dominican. With me there was the Servite, Fr Corr, and two consultors, Mgr Davis, our most experienced ecumenist, and Fr Bevenot, s.j. The English team was surprised by the ideas of some of our brethren. Their outlook on the Mass, for example, was startling. Some priests never offered Mass, being content to receive Holy Communion. To our relief the Council was to stress the importance to the priest of his daily Mass.

Our greatest difficulty was to give a picture of the Anglican Church. Most foreigners think that the Church of England is mainly Anglo-Catholic. As the only bishop in the Secretariat with a life-long experience of Anglicans, I was dismayed at the prospect of trying to teach my colleagues that Anglicans may also be Evangelicals or Modern Churchmen. There were two consultors from North America—Fr Tavard from the U.S.A., a Frenchman by birth, and Fr Baum from Canada, a German Jewish convert. Fortunately during the course of the Council many more bishops were appointed from the English-speaking countries.

I took my problem to Pope John. I had talked to him on a previous occasion about the difficulty of explaining to a foreigner the comprehensiveness of the Church of England. I explained why it was imperative for me to have the support of another English bishop. While I remained a lone voice the members of the Secretariat might well think that I was giving purely personal views of the religious situation in England. I asked that Bishop Holland (then auxiliary in Portsmouth) be nominated. The speed of his reaction to my request is a testimony to Pope John's efficiency. On the very next morning I was asked to call on Archbishop Felici the Secretary General of the impending Council. He needed biographical notes on the new candidate—a former professor of theology and no stranger to the work for Christian Unity. Before the week was out Bishop Holland was appointed a member of the Secretariat.

This epilogue is not an autobiography. I have already explained why it seemed useful to record the thoughts which came to me when I was apparently close to death. These thoughts presumably took their direction from my own preoccupations at the moment when I was struck down. For the purposes of this book I had been struggling to understand the attitude of the Catholic critics of the hierarchy. I was seriously trying to trace its origin. I made an honest attempt to discover if, as a member of the hierarchy, I had done anything to stimulate hostility. It was unlikely at such a moment that I would deceive myself. If in June I had been required to give an account of my stewardship of souls I would have been more anxious to confess my faults than to find excuses. My self-examination did not leave me with a sense of self-righteousness but before God I knew that lack of concern for people—the most common accusation made against the hierarchy—was very far down the long list of my sins.

I felt compassion for the Catholics who in masochistic

fashion make themselves miserable by continually denigrating their own Church. I pitied especially the hungry young sheep who refuse pasture because they have been told by their elders not to trust the shepherds. I thought with sorrow of the young, badly served by those placed by God to guide them. For their sake my indignation rose against parents too lazy or self-indulgent to check their children; against priests and teachers who betray the young by following instead of leading them. Such men and women fail the Church in whose name they act. The roots of their failure are a craving for the admiration of the young and a pathetic desire to recapture a lost youth. I felt genuine sympathy for the victims of delusions of intellectual grandeur but I recognized their great share of responsibility for the present unrest. I was too ill to be in patronizing mood. I thought how much less tormented these souls would be if in good conscience they could renounce the faith. But this they cannot do. They know that the Catholic Church is the fair bride of Christ. They are miserable because they believe that the Church is incompetently led. The critics are good men and women who sincerely believe the hard things they say about their Fathers in God. May God bless and guide us all!